Study Guide and Working Papers

Chapters 16-27

College Accounting

Twenty-third Edition

James A. Heintz, DBA, CPA
Professor of Accounting
School of Business
University of Kansas

Robert W. Parry, Jr., Ph.D.
Professor of Accounting
Kelley School of Business
Indiana University

Cengage

Australia • Brazil • Canada • Mexico • Singapore • United Kingdom • United States

Cengage

WCN: 01-100-1014

For product information and technology assistance, contact us at **Cengage Customer & Sales Support, 1-800-354-9706 or support.cengage.com.**

For permission to use material from this text or product, submit all requests online at **www.copyright.com**.

ISBN: 978-1-337-91357-7

Cengage
200 Pier 4 Boulevard
Boston, MA 02210
USA

Cengage is a leading provider of customized learning solutions with employees residing in nearly 40 different countries and sales in more than 125 countries around the world. Find your local representative at: **www.cengage.com.**

To learn more about Cengage platforms and services, register or access your online learning solution, or purchase materials for your course, visit **www.cengage.com.**

Table of Contents

Study Guide

Working Papers

CHAPTER 16
ACCOUNTING FOR ACCOUNTS RECEIVABLE

LEARNING OBJECTIVES

In Chapter 16, you will learn how to account for accounts receivable. Most businesses realize that sales will increase if customers are allowed credit. However, some customers are unable or unwilling to pay their accounts.

Objective 1. Apply the allowance method of accounting for uncollectible accounts.

The **allowance method** of accounting for uncollectible accounts receivable attempts to recognize **bad debt expense** in the same time period as the credit sales were made. This method is in conformity with the **matching principle**, which states that expenses should be matched with the revenues they helped to produce. To use the **allowance method**, three steps are followed.

1. At the end of each accounting period, the amount of **bad debt expense** or uncollectible accounts is estimated.
2. An adjusting entry is made to recognize the **bad debt expense** and reduce reported receivables for the amount of uncollectible accounts, as follows:

Bad Debt Expense	xx	
Allowance for Doubtful Accounts ...		xx

Notice, the credit above is to the allowance account, not to Accounts Receivable. The allowance account is deducted from Accounts Receivable to arrive at the **net receivables** or **net realizable value,** as follows:

Current assets:	
Accounts receivable	$50,000
Less allowance for doubtful accounts	5,000
Net realizable value	$45,000

3. When a specific account is identified as uncollectible, an entry is made to write off the account and reduce the balance in Allowance for Doubtful Accounts.

Allowance for Doubtful Accounts........	xx	
Accounts Receivable........................		xx

Objective 2. Apply the percentage of sales and percentage of receivables methods of estimating uncollectible accounts.

There are two basic approaches to using the **allowance method** to estimate the amount of uncollectibles: the percentage of sales method and the percentage of receivables method.

The **percentage of sales method** is based on the relationship between the amount of credit sales and the amount of uncollectible accounts experienced in prior years. An important feature of this method is that the balance in Allowance for Doubtful Accounts before adjustment is ignored in making the adjusting entry for Bad Debt Expense. In other words, the estimated percentage is multiplied by the year's credit sales, and this amount is then used in the adjusting entry. The only exception to this rule is when either a large debit balance or a large credit balance is accumulating from one year to the next in Allowance for Doubtful Accounts. This would indicate that the estimated percentage of credit sales is either too low or too high and needs to be increased or decreased.

The **percentage of receivables method** is based on the relationship between the amount of accounts receivable and the amount of uncollectible accounts experienced in prior years. Either an estimated percentage multiplied by the Accounts Receivable balance or an aging of the accounts receivable can be used to estimate uncollectible accounts. The aging analysis is a more precise method of estimating uncollectibles because it examines each customer's account to determine how long it has been outstanding.

An important feature of the **percentage of receivables method** is that you must examine the existing balance in Allowance for Doubtful Accounts before entering the adjusting entry. If the balance prior to adjustment is a debit, then this debit amount is *added* to the dollar estimate determined by the **percentage of receivables method**. If the balance prior to adjustment is a credit, then this credit amount is *subtracted* from the estimate determined by the **percentage of receivables method**.

Occasionally, an account that was written off will be collected. When this happens, two entries are required.

1. The account is reinstated as follows:

Accounts Receivable	xx	
Allowance for Doubtful Accounts .		xx

Notice that the above entry is the exact reverse of the write-off entry.

2. The collection is entered as follows:

Cash	xx	
Accounts Receivable......................		xx

Objective 3. Apply the direct write-off method of accounting for uncollectible accounts.

Under the **direct write-off method**, Bad Debt Expense is not recognized until it has been determined that an account is uncollectible. Thus, there is no end-of-period adjusting entry to estimate Bad Debt Expense. When an account is to be written off, Bad Debt Expense is debited and Accounts Receivable is credited.

There are three disadvantages to using this method. First, the **matching principle** will be violated if the account is written off in a time period different from the year the sale was made. Second, the amount of Bad Debt Expense recognized in a given period can be manipulated by management. Third, the amount of Accounts Receivable reported on the balance sheet overstates the amount of cash actually expected to be collected.

Occasionally, an account that was written off will be collected. If the collection is made in the same year as the sale was made, then a simple reversal of the write-off entry is made, along with an entry showing the cash collected.

Accounts Receivable	xx	
Bad Debt Expense..........................		xx
Cash	xx	
Accounts Receivable.....................		xx

If the write-off is made in one time period but the recovery is made in a following accounting period, then a different entry is required to reinstate the account.

Accounts Receivable	xx	
Uncollectible Accounts Recovered ..		xx

Notice in the above entry that the credit is to Uncollectible Accounts Recovered. This account is reported on the income statement as other revenue. The collection is recorded in the same manner as the previous example.

Cash	xx	
Accounts Receivable.......................		xx

REVIEW QUESTIONS

Instructions: Analyze each of the following items carefully before writing your answer in the column at the right.

	Question	Answer
LO 1	**1.** Name the two methods of accounting for uncollectible accounts.	____________________ ____________________
LO 1	**2.** The ________ method is a technique that attempts to recognize Bad Debt Expense in the same period that the related sales are made.	____________________
LO 1	**3.** The ________ principle states that expenses should be matched with the revenues they helped to produce.	____________________
LO 1	**4.** Under the accrual basis of accounting, the ________ method is generally required for financial reporting purposes.	____________________
LO 1	**5.** Using the allowance method, the end-of-period adjusting entry involves a debit to ________ and a credit to ________.	____________________ ____________________
LO 1	**6.** The account Allowance for Doubtful Accounts is classified on the balance sheet as a(n) ________.	____________________
LO 1	**7.** The dollar difference between Accounts Receivable and Allowance for Doubtful Accounts is known as ________.	____________________
LO 2	**8.** Name the two basic methods used under the allowance method to estimate the amount of uncollectibles.	____________________ ____________________
LO 2	**9.** The ________ method is based on the relationship between the amount of credit sales and the amount of uncollectible accounts experienced in prior years.	____________________
LO 2	**10.** Under the allowance method, when an account is written off as uncollectible, ________ is debited, and ________ is credited. ..	____________________ ____________________
LO 2	**11.** The ________ method is based on the relationship between the amount of accounts receivable and the amount of uncollectible accounts experienced in prior years.	____________________
LO 2	**12.** The process of analyzing each customer's balance to determine how long the account receivable has been outstanding is called _______.	____________________

LO 2 13. The existing balance in Allowance for Doubtful Accounts can be ignored when estimating uncollectible accounts under the ________ method. .... ____________________

LO 2 14. The existing balance in Allowance for Doubtful Accounts must be examined when estimating uncollectible accounts under the ________ method. .... ____________________

LO 2 15. Under the allowance method, to reinstate an account that had previously been written off, ________ is debited, and ________ is credited. .... ____________________

____

LO 2 16. To record the collection of an account that has been reinstated, ________ is debited, and ________ is credited. .... ____________________

____

LO 3 17. Under the ________ method, Bad Debt Expense is not recognized until it has been determined that an account is uncollectible. .... ____________________

LO 3 18. Under the direct write-off method, to reinstate an account in the same accounting period that the account was written off, the account ________ is credited. .... ____________________

LO 3 19. Under the direct write-off method, to reinstate an account that was written off in an earlier accounting period, the account ________ is credited. .... ____________________

LO 3 20. Under the direct write-off method, the account ________ is debited when writing off an uncollectible account. .... ____________________

EXERCISES

Exercise 1 (LO 1/2) UNCOLLECTIBLE ACCOUNTS—PERCENTAGE OF SALES; NET REALIZABLE VALUE

McAllister's Framing and Art Supplies uses the percentage of sales method of accounting for uncollectible accounts. At the end of 20-9, Sue McAllister estimates that uncollectible accounts associated with this year's sales will be approximately $3,500. The balances in related accounts just prior to entering adjusting entries are listed below. Prepare the appropriate adjusting entry on December 31, 20-9, and compute net realizable value.

	Debit	Credit
Accounts Receivable	28,000	
Allowance for Doubtful Accounts		300
Bad Debt Expense	-0-	

Exercise 1 (Concluded)

GENERAL JOURNAL PAGE

	DATE	DESCRIPTION	POST. REF.	DEBIT	CREDIT	
1						1
2						2
3						3

Exercise 2 (LO 1/2) UNCOLLECTIBLE ACCOUNTS—PERCENTAGE OF RECEIVABLES; NET REALIZABLE VALUE

Sherfield's Toy Shop uses the percentage of receivables method of accounting for uncollectible accounts. At the end of 20-6, Robert Sherfield estimates that there will be $3,200 worth of uncollectible accounts. The balances in related accounts just prior to entering adjusting entries are listed below. Prepare the appropriate adjusting entry on December 31, 20-6, and compute net realizable value.

	Debit	Credit
Accounts Receivable	32,000	
Allowance for Doubtful Accounts		400
Bad Debt Expense	-0-	

GENERAL JOURNAL PAGE

	DATE	DESCRIPTION	POST. REF.	DEBIT	CREDIT	
1						1
2						2
3						3

Exercise 3 (LO 2) COLLECTION OF ACCOUNT WRITTEN OFF—ALLOWANCE METHOD

Freeflow Pen Company uses the allowance method of accounting for uncollectible accounts. On November 15, 20-7, Beatrice Fountain's account was written off as uncollectible. At the time, Fountain owed $350. On January 21, 20-8, a check for $350 was received from Ms. Fountain. Prepare entries for the write-off on November 15, 20-7, and for receipt of the check on January 21, 20-8.

GENERAL JOURNAL PAGE

	DATE	DESCRIPTION	POST. REF.	DEBIT	CREDIT	
1						1
2						2
3						3
4						4
5						5
6						6
7						7
8						8
9						9
10						10
11						11
12						12

Exercise 4 (LO 3) DIRECT WRITE-OFF METHOD

Maui Surf and Sport Shop uses the direct write-off method of accounting for uncollectible accounts. On March 15, 20-8, a letter from Bill Karst was received stating that he had lost his job and would be unable to pay the $250 owed on account. Make the general journal entry necessary to write off Mr. Karst's account.

GENERAL JOURNAL PAGE

	DATE	DESCRIPTION	POST. REF.	DEBIT	CREDIT	
1						1
2						2
3						3

Exercise 5 (LO 3) COLLECTION OF ACCOUNT WRITTEN OFF—DIRECT WRITE-OFF METHOD

B. Q. Company uses the direct write-off method of accounting for uncollectible accounts. On November 15, 20-4, the two accounts listed below were written off as uncollectible.

Account	Amount
Brenda Farlow	$400
Charles Turner	500

On December 21, 20-4, a check was received from Farlow for $400; and on January 15, 20-5, a check for $500 was received from Turner. Prepare entries for the write-off of each account on November 15, 20-4, and for the receipt of the checks on December 21, 20-4, and January 15, 20-5. Assume that B. Q.'s fiscal year ends on December 31.

GENERAL JOURNAL PAGE

	DATE		DESCRIPTION	POST. REF.	DEBIT	CREDIT	
1							1
2							2
3							3
4							4
5							5
6							6
7							7
8							8
9							9
10							10
11							11
12							12
13							13
14							14
15							15
16							16
17							17
18							18
19							19
20							20
21							21
22							22
23							23
24							24
25							25
26							26

PROBLEMS

Problem 6 (LO 2) UNCOLLECTIBLE ACCOUNTS—PERCENTAGE OF SALES AND PERCENTAGE OF RECEIVABLES

At the end of the current year, the balance of the accounts receivable account for Webb's Pet Supplies was $32,000. Credit sales for the year were $450,800.

Required:

Determine the amount of the adjusting entry for uncollectible accounts and the net realizable value under each of the following assumptions:

(a) Allowance for Doubtful Accounts has a credit balance of $400.
  (1) The percentage of sales method is used, and it is estimated that bad debt expense will be 1% of credit sales.
  (2) The percentage of receivables method is used; and based on an analysis of the accounts, it is estimated that uncollectible accounts will amount to $4,250.

(b) Allowance for Doubtful Accounts has a debit balance of $600.
  (1) The percentage of sales method is used, and it is estimated that bad debt expense will be 1.5% of credit sales.
  (2) The percentage of receivables method is used; and based on an analysis of the accounts, it is estimated that uncollectible accounts will amount to $6,200.

(a) (1) ______________________________

(2) ______________________________

(b) (1) ______________________________

(2) ______________________________

Problem 7 (LO 2) UNCOLLECTIBLE ACCOUNTS—PERCENTAGE OF SALES; COLLECTION OF ACCOUNT WRITTEN OFF

Chattanooga Fireworks Company (CFC) uses the percentage of sales method of accounting for uncollectible accounts. In the past, approximately 2% of all credit sales have been uncollectible. Credit sales for 20-6 amounted to $850,000. At the end of 20-6, Accounts Receivable had a debit balance of $120,000, and Allowance for Doubtful Accounts had a credit balance of $1,500. The following transactions occurred in 20-7:

Mar.	1	Wrote off the account of J. Dullard for $380.
May	30	Received a check from J. Dullard for $380.

Required:

1. Enter the adjusting entry for bad debt expense at the end of 20-6.
2. Prepare journal entries for the transactions that occurred in 20-7.

GENERAL JOURNAL

PAGE

	DATE		DESCRIPTION	POST. REF.	DEBIT	CREDIT	
1							1
2							2
3							3
4							4
5							5
6							6
7							7
8							8
9							9
10							10
11							11
12							12
13							13
14							14
15							15
16							16

Problem 8 (LO 2) UNCOLLECTIBLE ACCOUNTS—AGING OF ACCOUNTS RECEIVABLE

Tallahassee Seminole Shop uses the percentage of receivables method of accounting for uncollectible accounts. An analysis of the accounts receivable ledger at the end of 20-9 reveals the following data concerning specific customers:

Customers	Invoice Dates and Amounts of Unpaid Invoices					
Borthick, A.	10/7	$2,300	11/15	$1,200	12/18	$3,000
Clark, R.	6/1	1,200	8/15	2,500		
Copley, P.	9/23	4,500	10/22	2,300	12/23	2,800
Davis, H.	12/15	1,500				
Heagy, C.	9/9	200				
O'Keefe, S.	11/20	3,300	12/10	1,400		
Pasewark, W.	12/2	5,500				
Schroeder, M.	12/15	2,300				
Shockley, W.	11/18	800	12/8	3,000		
Wilkerson, J.	8/21	300	11/15	1,100	12/8	1,700

At December 31, 20-9, the unadjusted balance in Allowance for Doubtful Accounts is a debit of $500. All sales are billed n/30. The chart below is used to estimate the uncollectibles using the aging of receivables method.

Days Past Due	Percent Uncollectible
Not yet due	2%
1–30 days	4
31–60 days	8
61–90 days	16
Over 90 days	32

Required:

1. Prepare an aging schedule. Headings for this have been provided on the following page.
2. Estimate the uncollectible accounts as of the end of 20-9.
3. Prepare the adjusting entry for uncollectible accounts, using the journal provided on the following page.

Problem 8 (Concluded)

1. and 2.

TALLAHASSEE SEMINOLE SHOP
AGING SCHEDULE OF ACCOUNTS RECEIVABLE

	A	B	C	D	E	F	G
1			Not Yet	Number of Days Past Due			
2	Customer	Total	Due	1–30	31–60	61–90	Over 90
3							
4							
5							
6							
7							
8							
9							
10							
11							
12							
13							
14							
15							
16							
17							
18							
19							
20							

3.

GENERAL JOURNAL PAGE

	DATE		DESCRIPTION	POST. REF.	DEBIT	CREDIT	
1							1
2							2
3							3

Problem 9 (LO 3) COLLECTION OF ACCOUNT WRITTEN OFF—DIRECT WRITE-OFF METHOD

Woodruff & Burnside Distributors uses the direct write-off method in accounting for uncollectible accounts. The following selected transactions occurred during 20-6 and 20-7:

20-6

Mar.	20	Sold merchandise on account to Ready Merchants, $19,400.
May	12	Sold merchandise on account to Neighborhood Watchers, $13,800.
July	9	Received $12,000 from Ready Merchants and wrote off the remainder owed on the sale of March 20 as uncollectible.
Oct.	15	Received $6,000 from Neighborhood Watchers and wrote off the remainder owed on the sale of May 12 as uncollectible.
Dec.	5	Reinstated the Ready Merchants' account that had been written off on July 9 and received $7,400 cash in full settlement.

20-7

Feb.	26	Reinstated the Neighborhood Watchers' account that had been written off on October 15 of the previous year and received $7,800 cash in full settlement.

Required:

Record the above transactions in general journal form.

GENERAL JOURNAL

PAGE

DATE		DESCRIPTION	POST. REF.	DEBIT	CREDIT

Problem 9 (Concluded)

GENERAL JOURNAL

PAGE

DATE		DESCRIPTION	POST. REF.	DEBIT	CREDIT

CHAPTER 17
ACCOUNTING FOR NOTES AND INTEREST

LEARNING OBJECTIVES

Chapter 17 covers the giving and receiving of promissory notes as a part of the receivable and payable processes. Interest and due dates are calculated, followed by notes receivable and notes payable transactions. Accrued interest on notes receivable and notes payable is also calculated, and adjusting entries are illustrated.

Objective 1. Describe a promissory note.

A **promissory note** is a written promise to pay a specific sum at a future date. It is a legal, negotiable instrument used to extend time for payment or to allow borrowing of money for a specific period of time.

Objective 2. Calculate interest on and determine the due date of promissory notes.

To calculate interest, the formula **Interest = P × R × T** is used, where *P* is **principal of the note**; *R* is **rate of interest**; and *T* is **time** of the note, which is stated as a fraction of a year. The denominator of the fraction is 360 for days or 12 for months. Days of a loan are calculated by subtracting the date of the loan from the number of days in the month of issue and counting days forward in subsequent months to the **maturity date**. **Maturity value** is the principal plus interest for the length of the loan.

Objective 3. Account for notes receivable transactions and accrued interest.

Businesses other than banks and savings and loans generally encounter seven types of transactions involving notes receivable.

1. Note received from a customer in exchange for assets sold
2. Note received from a customer to extend time for payment of an account
3. Note collected at maturity
4. Note renewed at maturity
5. Note discounted before maturity
6. Note dishonored
7. Collection of dishonored note

When a note is discounted at a bank before maturity, the discount is based on the maturity value of the note, not the principal amount. If a note is **dishonored**, the **payee** transfers the amount of the note plus interest and any bank fees to accounts receivable. If a dishonored note is collected, the payee normally receives the maturity value of the note plus any bank fees and interest for the period from the original maturity date to the final collection date.

Recognition of revenue when it is earned (accrual accounting) requires that **accrued interest** (earned but not received) should be recognized at the end of the accounting period. Total accrued interest is debited to Accrued Interest Receivable and credited to Interest Revenue.

Objective 4. Account for notes payable transactions and accrued interest.

Businesses generally encounter five types of transactions involving notes payable.

1. Note issued to a supplier in exchange for assets purchased
2. Note issued to a supplier to extend time for payment of an account
3. Note issued as security for cash loan
4. Note paid at maturity
5. Note renewed at maturity

Banks often deduct interest in advance on a loan using a procedure called **discounting**. The bank issues a **non-interest-bearing note** and deducts a bank discount from the maturity value of the note. The borrower receives the **proceeds**, which are equal to the difference between the maturity value of the note and the discount amount. The effective **interest rate** on such notes is higher than the stated rate.

Under accrual accounting, expenses are recognized when they are incurred, rather than when they are paid. Therefore, **accrued interest** (due but not paid) should be recognized at the end of the accounting period. Total accrued interest is debited to Interest Expense and credited to Accrued Interest Payable or Discount on Notes Payable.

REVIEW QUESTIONS

Instructions: Analyze each of the following items carefully before writing your answer in the column at the right.

		Question	Answer
LO 1	**1.**	A(n) ________ is a written promise to pay a specific sum at a definite future date.	________________
LO 1	**2.**	The ________ signs the note and agrees to make payment.	________________
LO 1	**3.**	The note is payable to a specific person or business known as the ________.	________________
LO 2	**4.**	The ________ of a note is the face amount that will be paid at maturity.	________________
LO 2	**5.**	The rate of ________ is expressed as a percentage such as 7%.	________________
LO 2	**6.**	Most notes are usually expressed in months or days from the date of issue to the date of maturity, known as the ________ of the note.	________________
LO 2	**7.**	________ is the term of a note, stated as a fraction of a year.	________________
LO 2	**8.**	________ is the principal of a note plus the interest.	________________
LO 3	**9.**	When a note is given by a customer to extend time for payment, ________ is credited.	________________
LO 3	**10.**	When a note is collected by a bank, the payee receives a(n) ________ indicating the net amount added to the account.	________________
LO 3	**11.**	If a firm needs cash before a note receivable is due, it can endorse the note and transfer it to the bank for collection. This is called ________ a note receivable.	________________
LO 3	**12.**	The bank charges a fee called a(n) ________ for the time between the date of discounting and the maturity date of a note.	________________
LO 3	**13.**	The difference between the maturity value of the note and the bank discount is called the ________.	________________
LO 3	**14.**	The business still has ________ liability for a note that has been discounted at a bank.	________________
LO 3	**15.**	If the maker of a note does not pay or renew a note at maturity, the note is said to be ________.	________________

LO 3 16. When a note is dishonored, ________ is debited for the full maturity value of the note. .... ____________________

LO 3 17. A business that has many notes from customers would keep a(n) ________ register, which is an auxiliary record. .... ____________________

LO 3 18. The information contained in the notes receivable register is directly from the __________. .... ____________________

LO 3 19. At the end of the period, interest earned but not yet due is called ________ interest receivable. .... ____________________

LO 4 20. When banks make loans using non-interest-bearing notes, they subtract interest in advance. This procedure is called _______. ____________________

LO 4 21. Discount on Notes Payable is a(n) ________ account and is reported as a deduction from Notes Payable on the balance sheet. ____________________

LO 4 22. ________ on notes payable is interest expense that has been incurred but not paid. .... ____________________

LO 4 23. Accrued interest payable is reported as a(n) ________ on the balance sheet. .... ____________________

EXERCISES

Exercise 1 (LO 2) TERM OF A NOTE

From the information given below, compute the *time in days* of the following notes. (Assume there are 28 days in February.)

Date of Note	Due Date	Time in Days
June 4	August 11	________
May 13	July 10	________
January 15	March 21	________
August 10	November 12	________
December 15	February 1	________
April 1	July 1	________

Exercise 2 (LO 2) DETERMINING DUE DATE

From the information given below, determine the *due date* of the following notes. (Assume there are 28 days in February.)

Date of Note	Term of Note	Due Date
February 1	45 days	________
May 11	60 days	________
March 18	90 days	________
June 1	30 days	________
December 15	55 days	________
October 31	120 days	________

Exercise 3 (LO 2) CALCULATING INTEREST

Using 360 days as the denominator, calculate interest for the following promissory notes using the formula $I = P \times R \times T$.

Principal	Rate	Time	Interest
$1,500	5%	45 days	________
3,000	6%	60 days	________
7,500	7%	90 days	________
2,800	8.8%	30 days	________
4,200	5.5%	88 days	________
1,990	7.9%	120 days	________

Exercise 4 (LO 2/3) NOTES RECEIVABLE ENTRIES

Prepare general journal entries for the following notes receivable transactions. Assume a 360-day year and 28 days in February.

Jan.	2	Received a \$3,000, 6%, 30-day note from J. Smith in payment for sale of merchandise.
	15	Received a \$2,500, 5%, 30-day note from K. Jones in payment of an accounts receivable balance.
Feb.	1	Received \$15 interest on the J. Smith note; the old note is renewed for 30 days at 6.5%.
	14	Received \$500 principal, plus interest on the K. Jones note; the old note is renewed for 30 days at 6%.
Mar.	3	Received principal and interest on the Smith note.
	16	Received principal and interest on the Jones note.

GENERAL JOURNAL

PAGE

DATE	DESCRIPTION	POST. REF.	DEBIT	CREDIT

Exercise 5 (LO 2/3) NOTES RECEIVABLE DISCOUNTING AND DISHONORED

Prepare general journal entries for the following notes receivable transactions. Assume a 360-day year.

Apr.	1	Received a 90-day, 6.5% note in payment for accounts receivable balance of $5,000.
	20	Discounted the note at a rate of 7%.
May	2	Received a 60-day, 6% note in payment for accounts receivable balance of $3,500.
July	1	The $3,500 note is dishonored.
Aug.	15	The dishonored note is collected, plus interest at 6% on the maturity value.

GENERAL JOURNAL

PAGE

DATE		DESCRIPTION	POST. REF.	DEBIT	CREDIT

Exercise 6 (LO 4) NOTES PAYABLE ENTRIES

Prepare general journal entries for the following notes payable transactions. Assume a 360-day year and 28 days in February.

Jan.	11	Gave a $5,000, 6%, 30-day note to extend payment on accounts payable to G. Adams.
	20	Gave a $3,000, 6%, 60-day note to Roy Co. for purchase of merchandise.
Feb.	10	Paid $500 cash, plus interest, to G. Adams to extend the note for an additional 30 days at 6%.
Mar.	12	Paid the G. Adams note in full.
	21	Paid the Roy Co. note in full.

GENERAL JOURNAL

PAGE

DATE	DESCRIPTION	POST. REF.	DEBIT	CREDIT

Exercise 7 (LO 4) ENTRIES FOR BORROWING USING NOTES PAYABLE

Prepare general journal entries for the following notes payable transactions. Assume a 360-day year.

Apr.	1	Borrowed $5,000, giving a 60-day, 6% note.
May	1	Borrowed $6,000, giving a 90-day non-interest-bearing note. The note is discounted 7% by the bank.
May	31	Paid the $5,000, 60-day, 6% note.
July	30	Paid the $6,000 non-interest-bearing note, recognizing the discount as interest expense.

GENERAL JOURNAL

PAGE

	DATE	DESCRIPTION	POST. REF.	DEBIT	CREDIT	
1						1
2						2
3						3
4						4
5						5
6						6
7						7
8						8
9						9
10						10
11						11
12						12
13						13
14						14
15						15
16						16
17						17
18						18

Exercise 8 (LO 3/4) ACCRUED INTEREST JOURNAL ENTRIES

At the end of the year, accrued interest on notes receivable and payable has been determined as shown below. Record the appropriate adjusting entries for accrued interest receivable and payable in the general journal.

(a) Accrued interest on outstanding notes receivable	$37.50
(b) Accrued interest on outstanding notes payable	71.10

GENERAL JOURNAL

PAGE

	DATE		DESCRIPTION	POST. REF.	DEBIT	CREDIT	
1							1
2							2
3							3
4							4
5							5
6							6
7							7

PROBLEMS

Problem 9 (LO 3) NOTES RECEIVABLE ENTRIES

Required:

Prepare general journal entries for the following notes receivable transactions of Lill Co.:

Mar.	1	Received a $1,400, 90-day, 5% note for sale of merchandise.
	13	Received a $2,000, 30-day, 5.5% note from H. Jelinek to extend time for payment of account receivable.
	29	Note received on March 1 is discounted at Kaw Bank at a discount rate of 6%.
Apr.	12	H. Jelinek paid the interest due on her note (see March 13) plus $400 on the principal and gives a new $1,600, 30-day, 6% note.
May	12	H. Jelinek paid the note issued April 12, plus interest.
	30	Note discounted at Kaw Bank on March 29 is dishonored. Lill Co. pays the bank the maturity value of the note plus a $30 bank fee.
June	29	The note dishonored on May 30 is collected. Lill Co. receives the maturity value of the note, the $30 bank fee, and interest at 6% on the maturity value and the bank fee.

Problem 9 (Concluded)

GENERAL JOURNAL

PAGE

	DATE	DESCRIPTION	POST. REF.	DEBIT	CREDIT	
1						1
2						2
3						3
4						4
5						5
6						6
7						7
8						8
9						9
10						10
11						11
12						12
13						13
14						14
15						15
16						16
17						17
18						18
19						19
20						20
21						21
22						22
23						23
24						24
25						25
26						26
27						27
28						28
29						29
30						30
31						31
32						32
33						33
34						34

Problem 10 (LO 4) NOTES PAYABLE ENTRIES

Required:

Prepare general journal entries for the following notes payable transactions of S. Maghanti Co.:

May	1	Issued a $4,000, 60-day, 7% note to a supplier for purchase of merchandise.
	20	Issued a $1,500, 30-day, 7% note in payment of an account payable.
	31	Borrowed $5,000 cash from the bank, giving a 60-day non-interest-bearing note, discounted at 6% by the bank.
June	19	Paid the $1,500 note issued on May 20, plus interest.
	30	Paid $1,000 plus interest and issued a new note for $3,000 to satisfy the $4,000 note issued on May 1.
July	15	Borrowed $3,000 cash from the bank, giving a 60-day, 6% note.
	30	Paid $5,000 to the bank in payment of the note issued on May 31.

GENERAL JOURNAL

PAGE

	DATE		DESCRIPTION	POST. REF.	DEBIT	CREDIT	
1							1
2							2
3							3
4							4
5							5
6							6
7							7
8							8
9							9
10							10
11							11
12							12
13							13
14							14
15							15
16							16
17							17
18							18
19							19
20							20
21							21
22							22
23							23
24							24
25							25
26							26

Problem 10 (Concluded)

GENERAL JOURNAL

PAGE

	DATE	DESCRIPTION	POST. REF.	DEBIT	CREDIT	
1						1
2						2
3						3
4						4
5						5
6						6
7						7
8						8

Problem 11 (LO 3/4) ACCRUED INTEREST RECEIVABLE AND PAYABLE

Required:

Calculate the amount of accrued interest receivable and payable and record the adjusting entries in the general journal.

(a) At the end of the year, interest is earned but not yet received on the following notes:
90-day, $1,500, 6% note dated December 1, 20-- .... ________
60-day, $3,000, 5% note dated December 10, 20-- .... ________
45-day, $2,000, 5.5% note dated November 30, 20-- .... ________

(b) At the end of the year, interest expense is incurred but not yet paid on the following notes:
45-day, $2,500, 5.5% note dated December 3, 20-- .... ________
65-day, $1,000, 7% note dated November 25, 20-- .... ________
90-day, $5,000, 6% note dated December 13, 20-- .... ________

GENERAL JOURNAL

PAGE

	DATE	DESCRIPTION	POST. REF.	DEBIT	CREDIT	
1						1
2						2
3						3
4						4
5						5
6						6
7						7
8						8

CHAPTER 18
ACCOUNTING FOR LONG-TERM ASSETS

LEARNING OBJECTIVES

Chapter 18 addresses accounting for the acquisition, depreciation, and disposal of property, plant, and equipment. Four depreciation methods for financial reporting purposes are illustrated along with methods used for tax purposes. Methods of disposing of assets include disposal, sale at a gain or loss, and exchanges of similar assets at a gain or loss. In addition, accounting procedures for natural resources and intangible assets are illustrated.

Objective 1. Determine the cost of property, plant, and equipment.

The **cost** of **long-term assets (property, plant, and equipment)** includes amounts spent to acquire and prepare them for their intended use. Long-term assets are entered into the accounting system by debiting asset accounts. Land improvements that are not permanent in nature are normally debited to a land improvements account.

Objective 2. Explain the nature and purpose of depreciation.

Depreciation is used to match the cost of **plant assets** with the revenues those assets help to produce. The adjustment involves debiting an expense—Depreciation Expense—that is reported on the income statement. The credit is to Accumulated Depreciation—a contra-asset account. When accumulated depreciation is subtracted from the original cost of the asset, the result is undepreciated cost or **book value**. This is a process of cost allocation, not valuation of the asset.

Objective 3. Compute depreciation using the straight-line, declining-balance, sum-of-the-years'-digits, units-of-production, and MACRS depreciation methods.

The **straight-line method** is calculated by subtracting **salvage value** from original cost and dividing by **useful life**. This method allocates an equal amount of depreciation to each year of useful life of the asset.

The **declining-balance method** depreciates an asset faster than the straight-line method. With double-declining-balance, the rate is twice the straight-line rate. For example, an asset with a useful life of five years would have a straight-line rate of 20% (100% divided by 5). With the **double-declining-balance method**, each year's depreciation is 40% of the asset's book value (declining balance) at the beginning of the period. An asset cannot be depreciated below its salvage value.

The **sum-of-the-years'-digits method,** like the declining-balance method, recognizes more depreciation in earlier years. The **depreciable cost** is multiplied by a fraction whose denominator is the sum of the years' digits. For example, the denominator for an asset with a five-year useful life would be 5 + 4 + 3 + 2 + 1 = 15. The numerator is the number of years of remaining life, taken from the beginning of the year. For an asset with a five-year life, the first year's depreciation would be 5/15 times the cost minus salvage value; the second year's depreciation, 4/15 times cost minus salvage, and so on.

The **units-of-production method** depreciates an asset to the extent that it was used during the year. First, you calculate a rate for charging usage. To do this, the original cost minus salvage value is divided by the expected output or total units that can be produced. For example, a truck that costs $10,000, had a salvage value of $2,000, and estimated miles of service of 80,000 would be $8,000 divided by 80,000, or $0.10 a mile. If the truck was driven 10,000 miles, the year's depreciation would be 10,000 times $0.10, or $1,000.

The **Modified Accelerated Cost Recovery System (MACRS)** may be used for tax purposes. The IRS provides depreciation rate schedules for use with various classes of property. See Figure 18-3 in the text. Simply find the appropriate rate based on the age of the asset and asset class in the IRS schedule, then multiply by the asset's original cost.

Businesses are also able to immediately expense 100% of the cost of qualified assets (not buildings) acquired and placed in service after September 27, 2017.

Objective 4. Account for repairs, maintenance, additions, improvements, and replacements to plant and equipment.

Expenditures for normal repairs and maintenance of plant and equipment are debited to Repairs Expense and reported on the income statement. Expenditures for all **additions** and **improvements (betterments)** that increase the usefulness of the buildings or equipment are debited to the appropriate asset account and therefore increase **book value**. Since these additions and improvements will provide future benefits, depreciation will be recognized. A **replacement** is when a component of a plant asset is replaced with a similar component. Replacements that extend the asset's useful life, but do not increase its usefulness or efficiency, are *debited* to Accumulated Depreciation. This decreases the amount of accumulated depreciation and therefore increases **book value**.

Objective 5. Account for the disposition of property, plant, and equipment.

Plant assets can be discarded (retired), sold, or exchanged for another asset. Regardless of method of disposal, it must be determined whether there was a gain or a loss. If the market value of the old asset is greater than its book value, a gain has occurred. If the market value is less than its book value, a loss has occurred. Losses are often recognized when an asset is discarded. Gains and losses are recognized when assets are sold or exchanged.

Objective 6. Explain the nature of, purpose of, and accounting for depletion.

Natural resources are accounted for as they are consumed—a process similar to the units-of-production method of computing depreciation. The cost of the property less salvage value is divided by the number of units of output the property contains to determine the **depletion** expense per unit. This rate, multiplied by the number of units removed and sold, is the depletion expense for the period.

Objective 7. Explain the nature of and accounting for intangible assets.

Intangible assets include valuable legal or economic rights that a firm may acquire. These include **patents**, **copyrights**, **trademarks**, **franchises**, and **goodwill**. Intangible assets with definite lives are amortized (written off) as yearly operating expenses. Those with indefinite lives are not amortized. All are tested for **impairment** on a regular basis. Property, plant, equipment, and intangible assets are considered impaired when the fair market value of the asset is less than the book value reported on the balance sheet. The details of the impairment tests are addressed in more advanced texts.

REVIEW QUESTIONS

Instructions: Analyze each of the following items carefully before writing your answer in the column at the right.

	Question	Answer
LO 1	**1.** Assets expected to provide benefits for a number of accounting periods are called ________ assets.	____________________
LO 1	**2.** Long-term assets that are ________ have physical substance. ...	____________________
LO 1	**3.** All long-term assets, except ________, gradually wear out or are used up as time passes.	____________________
LO 1	**4.** Land, buildings, furniture, and equipment are called ________, plant assets, or fixed assets.	____________________
LO 1	**5.** The cash ________ is the amount of cash that could have been paid to satisfy a supplier on the date of purchase of an asset.	____________________

LO 2 6. Depreciation is a process of cost ______, not a process of valuation. .... ______________

LO 2 7. The loss of usefulness because of deterioration from age and wear is called ________ depreciation. .... ______________

LO 2 8. The loss of usefulness because of inadequacy or obsolescence is called ________ depreciation. .... ______________

LO 3 9. For plant assets, the portion of an asset's cost recognized as an expense is called ________. .... ______________

LO 3 10. An estimate of how long an asset will be in service is called _______. .... ______________

LO 3 11. Estimated scrap, trade-in, or ________ value is what an asset is expected to be worth at the end of its useful life. .... ______________

LO 3 12. ________ is the original cost less scrap value. .... ______________

LO 3 13. Book value, or ________, represents cost less accumulated depreciation. .... ______________

LO 3 14. Under the ________ method, the depreciable cost of an asset is allocated equally over each year of useful life. .... ______________

LO 3 15. Under the ________ method, the book value is multiplied by a fixed rate; depreciation expense declines each year. .... ______________

LO 3 16. Under the ________ method, depreciation each year is determined by multiplying the depreciable base by a schedule of fractions. ______________

LO 3 17. Under the ________ method, depreciation is based on the extent to which the asset was used during the year. .... ______________

LO 4 18. Improvements to equipment that increase usefulness are debited to the ________ account. .... ______________

LO 4 19. Replacements to equipment that extend useful life but do not increase usefulness are debited to the ________ account. .... ______________

LO 6 20. As natural resources are removed, the expense is called ________. .... ______________

LO 6 21. Natural resources, often called ________ assets, are consumed in the operation of the business. .... ______________

LO 7 22. A(n) ________ is a grant by the federal government to an inventor giving the exclusive right to produce, use, and sell an invention. ______________

LO 7 23. A(n) ________ is the exclusive right to reproduction and sale of a literary, artistic, or musical composition. .... ______________

LO 7 24. A(n) ________ is a registered name that protects the owner by preventing others from using it. .... ______________

LO 7 25. A ________ is a contract under which a franchisor grants the franchisee the rights to sell products or services and to use trademarks or trade names under specified conditions. .... ____________________

LO 7 26. The excess of the amount paid for a company (market value of the company) and the market value of the company's net assets (assets – liabilities) is called ___________. .... ____________________

LO 7 27. An intangible asset is considered ________________ when the fair market value of the asset is less than the book value reported on the balance sheet. .... ____________________

EXERCISES

Exercise 1 (LO 1) COST OF PROPERTY, PLANT, AND EQUIPMENT

Joe Schultz, Inc., purchased six acres of land for $30,000. Mr. Schultz is uncertain about what other expenditures in relation to this purchase he should include in the cost of land. From the following list, choose what expenditures Mr. Schultz should include and total them.

Purchase price	$30,000
Legal fees related to purchase	1,000
Removal of old warehouse	8,000
Planting shrubs along road	1,500
Interest on loan to purchase property	3,000
Realtor fee	1,200

Exercise 2 (LO 3) STRAIGHT-LINE DEPRECIATION

Assume an asset purchased January 1, 20--, costs $5,000, has an expected life of five years, and has an expected salvage value of $500. Using the straight-line method, compute depreciation for each year.

Exercise 3 (LO 3) DOUBLE-DECLINING-BALANCE DEPRECIATION

Assume an asset cost $11,000 and was purchased on January 1, 20--. The asset is assumed to have a useful life of five years and a salvage value of $1,000. Using the double-declining-balance method, compute depreciation expense for each year.

Exercise 4 (LO 3) SUM-OF-THE-YEARS'-DIGITS DEPRECIATION

Assume an asset costing $7,900 was purchased on September 17, 20-1. The asset is assumed to have a useful life of five years and a salvage value of $400. Using the sum-of-the-years'-digits method, compute depreciation expense for each year, 20-1 to 20-6. Remember, assets acquired after the fifteenth are not depreciated until the next month.

Exercise 5 (LO 3) UNITS-OF-PRODUCTION DEPRECIATION

Assume an asset costing $9,000 was purchased January 1, 20--. The asset is assumed to produce 34,000 units and have a salvage value of $500. The first year, 12,000 units were produced; the second year, 8,000 units; the third year, 14,000 units. Using the units-of-production method, compute depreciation expense for each year.

Exercise 6 (LO 4) JOURNAL ENTRIES: REPAIRS, MAINTENANCE, ADDITIONS, IMPROVEMENTS, AND REPLACEMENTS

Enter the following transactions for the Ramirez Brothers' Garage in a general journal:

1. Changed oil in reservoir on Hydraulic Lift #1 (normal maintenance) for $50, cash.
2. Replaced compressor on Hydraulic Lift #2 for $600, cash. This will extend the lift's life.
3. Added another master cylinder to Hydraulic Lift #2 so large trucks could be repaired for $1,000, cash.

GENERAL JOURNAL PAGE

	DATE		DESCRIPTION	POST. REF.	DEBIT	CREDIT	
1							1
2							2
3							3
4							4
5							5
6							6
7							7
8							8
9							9
10							10

Exercise 7 (LO 6) DEPLETION

Assume a nickel mine is acquired at a cost of $400,000,000. No salvage value is expected. The estimated amount of nickel to be recovered is 16,000 tons. The first year, 800 tons of nickel are mined; the second year, 1,200 tons; the third year, 750 tons. Compute the depletion expense for each year.

PROBLEMS

Problem 8 (LO 3) STRAIGHT-LINE, SUM-OF-THE-YEARS'-DIGITS, DOUBLE-DECLINING-BALANCE, AND MACRS METHODS

Blockmaster Building Supplies purchased a truck on January 1, 20--, at a cost of $18,000. The estimated life of the truck is five years, and it is expected to have a salvage value of $3,000.

Required:

1. Compute depreciation expense and book value for each year using the following methods:
   (a) Straight-line
   (b) Sum-of-the-years'-digits
   (c) Double-declining-balance
2. Compute MACRS depreciation for each year of the asset's life. Assume the truck is a five year class of property.

1. (a)

Year	Depreciation Expense	Book Value
1		
2		
3		
4		
5		

1. (b)

Year	Depreciation Expense	Book Value
1		
2		
3		
4		
5		

1. (c)

Year	Depreciation Expense	Book Value
1		
2		
3		
4		
5		

Problem 8 (LO 3) (Concluded)

2.

Year	Depreciation Expense
1	
2	
3	
4	
5	
6	

Problem 9 (LO3/4) DEPRECIATION, IMPROVEMENTS, AND REPLACEMENTS

On January 1, 20-1, two sonar systems were purchased by Sea Treasures, Inc., for $4,000 each with a salvage value of $400 and estimated lives of six years. On January 1, 20-2, a computer chip was replaced on Sonar System #1 for $200 cash. The computer chip will extend the life of System #1 by three years. The transducer in Sonar System #2 was upgraded for $1,000 cash with a more sensitive one to improve the possibility of finding a treasure.

Required:

1. Using the straight-line method, journalize the entries for depreciation on December 31, 20-1, for Sonar Systems #1 and #2 in a general journal.

GENERAL JOURNAL PAGE

	DATE		DESCRIPTION	POST. REF.	DEBIT	CREDIT	
1							1
2							2
3							3
4							4
5							5
6							6
7							7
8							8
9							9

Problem 9 (Concluded)

2. Enter the transactions for January 20-2 in a general journal.

GENERAL JOURNAL PAGE

	DATE		DESCRIPTION	POST. REF.	DEBIT	CREDIT	
1							1
2							2
3							3
4							4
5							5
6							6
7							7
8							8
9							9

3. Assuming no other improvements or replacements, compute depreciation expense for each sonar system for 20-2 through 20-6.

Problem 10 (LO 5) DISPOSITION OF ASSETS

The following assets are disposed of by XYZ Construction Company:

Jan.	5	Backhoe that cost $85,000 and had accumulated depreciation of $85,000 was discarded.
	28	Truck that cost $28,000 and had accumulated depreciation of $27,200 was sold for $1,000.
Feb.	10	Handtruck that cost $2,500 and had accumulated depreciation of $2,200 was sold for $150.

The following assets are exchanged or traded in by XYZ Construction Company:

Mar.	11	A forklift that had a cost of $50,000 and accumulated depreciation of $45,000 was traded in for a new forklift with a fair market value of $60,000. The old forklift and $55,000 in cash were given for the new forklift.
May	16	A caterpillar that had a cost of $105,000 and accumulated depreciation of $90,000 was traded in for a new caterpillar with a fair market value of $120,000. The old caterpillar and $110,000 in cash were given for the new caterpillar.
June	10	A dump truck that had a cost of $80,000 and accumulated depreciation of $78,000 was traded in for a new dump truck with a fair market value of $90,000. The old truck and $87,000 cash were given for the new truck.

Required:

Prepare journal entries, using a general journal.

Problem 10 (Concluded)

GENERAL JOURNAL

PAGE

	DATE	DESCRIPTION	POST. REF.	DEBIT	CREDIT	
1						1
2						2
3						3
4						4
5						5
6						6
7						7
8						8
9						9
10						10
11						11
12						12
13						13
14						14
15						15
16						16
17						17
18						18
19						19
20						20
21						21
22						22
23						23
24						24
25						25
26						26
27						27
28						28
29						29

Problem 11 (LO 6) ACCOUNTING FOR DEPLETION

Kramer Diamond Mining Company purchased land and mining rights for $105 million. The residual value of the land is expected to be $5 million. The mine is expected to produce 10 million karats and will be depleted based on the number of karats mined each period.

Required:

1. Compute depletion expense for the following years:

20-1	4.0 million karats mined and sold
20-2	3.5 million karats mined and sold
20-3	2.0 million karats mined and sold

2. Prepare the entries to record the depletion, using a general journal.

GENERAL JOURNAL

PAGE

	DATE		DESCRIPTION	POST. REF.	DEBIT	CREDIT	
1							1
2							2
3							3
4							4
5							5
6							6
7							7
8							8
9							9

Problem 12 (LO 7) INTANGIBLE LONG-TERM ASSETS

Product Innovation and Development Company purchased the following intangible assets:

Jan.	4	Patent with an estimated useful life of eight years at a cost of $12,000 (Patent #1).
Mar.	18	Patent with an estimated useful life of five years at a cost of $15,000 (Patent #2).
May	11	Copyright for $22,000 with a legal life on the copyright of 14 years, but an estimated economic life of eight years (round to two decimal places).
Oct.	1	Signed a 10-year franchise agreement and opened a Geeky Group high tech service company. Paid $200,000 to the franchisor.

Required:

Record this year's amortization expense, using a general journal. Assume straight-line amortization.

GENERAL JOURNAL

PAGE

	DATE	DESCRIPTION	POST. REF.	DEBIT	CREDIT	
1						1
2						2
3						3
4						4
5						5
6						6
7						7
8						8
9						9
10						10
11						11
12						12

CHAPTER 19
ACCOUNTING FOR PARTNERSHIPS

LEARNING OBJECTIVES

Chapter 19 introduces you to the important features and accounting procedures of the partnership form of business. You will learn how to account for the formation, dissolution, and liquidation of a partnership. In addition, you will learn how partners are compensated and how to report partner compensation and the allocation of net income.

Objective 1. Describe the various types of partnerships, their characteristics, the partnership agreement, and the advantages and disadvantages of a partnership.

A **partnership** is composed of two or more individuals engaged in business as co-owners. The partnership form of business includes the following types:

General Partnership—A partnership made up of **general partners** who actively participate in the management of the business and are personally liable for all debts of the partnership.
Limited Partnership (LP)—A partnership with at least one general partner with responsibilities of managing the firm and who is subject to **unlimited liability**. **Limited partners** simply invest funds and do not participate in management decisions. Their liability is limited to the amount invested.
Limited Liability Partnership (LLP)—A partnership in which all partners may actively participate in the management of the firm, but whose personal liability is limited to their own actions and the actions of those they supervise.

The characteristics of partnerships include:

1. Co-ownership of assets
2. **Mutual agency**
3. Limited life
4. Unlimited liability
5. No federal income tax

A **partnership agreement** includes the following:

1. Date of agreement
2. Names of the partners
3. Kind of business to be conducted
4. Length of time the partnership is to run
5. Name and location of the business
6. Investment of each partner
7. Basis on which profits or losses are to be shared by the partners
8. Limitation of partners' rights and activities
9. Salary allowances to partners
10. Division of assets upon dissolution of the partnership
11. Signatures of the partners

Advantages:
Combined experience of partners
Increased ability to raise capital
Improved credit standing

(continued)

Disadvantages:
- Unlimited liability of general partners
- Mutual agency
- Difficulty transferring the interests of partners to others
- Various events can cause the partnership to be dissolved

Objective 2. Prepare entries for the initial investments in a partnership.

A partnership may be formed by the investment of cash and/or other assets by the partners. The fair market value of each partner's assets is used when accounting for the formation of the partnership. When partnerships are formed from existing businesses, their respective balance sheets serve as the basis for the opening entries for the investments of such partners.

Objective 3. Explain how partners are compensated and account for the allocation of net income.

The basis on which profits and losses are shared is a matter of agreement among the partners. In the absence of any agreement among the partners, profits and losses must be shared equally. Each partner has his or her own drawing account and capital account. After revenues and expenses have been closed to the income summary account at the end of the accounting period, Income Summary is closed by allocating each partner's share of net income or loss to his or her individual capital account. This allocation of net income may be based on a **salary allowance** provided to each partner, and/or **interest allowance** on beginning capital investments, and/or by a predetermined ratio, or by any other prearranged agreement among the partners.

Objective 4. Prepare financial statements reporting the allocation of net income and partnership equity.

The allocation of net income and its impact on the partners' capital balances should be disclosed in the financial statements. All three financial statements are affected: the income statement, statement of partners' equity, and the balance sheet.

Objective 5. Describe the actions that result in the dissolution of a partnership and account for the dissolution.

Dissolution of a partnership may be brought about through the addition of a new partner, the death or withdrawal of one of the partners, or bankruptcy. Dissolution of the partnership does not always mean that business operations will cease. A dissolution may mean that the old partnership agreement is invalid, and a new partnership agreement must be created because of one or more of the above mentioned reasons.

By agreement, a partner may retire and be permitted to withdraw assets equal to, less than, or greater than the amount of the retiring partner's capital interest in the partnership. If a retiring partner agrees to withdraw less than or more than the amount accumulated in his or her capital account, the effect of the transaction will either increase or decrease the capital accounts of the remaining partners.

Objective 6. Describe how a partnership is liquidated and prepare associated entries and a statement of partnership liquidation.

Liquidation of a partnership generally means that the assets are sold, gains and losses are allocated to partners, liabilities are paid, and the remaining cash or other assets are distributed to the partners. If there is a gain or loss on the sale of the noncash assets, this gain or loss is allocated to the partners' capital accounts based on their profit-and-loss sharing ratio. Once all liabilities are paid, the remaining cash is distributed to the partners according to their ownership interests as indicated by the balances of their capital accounts.

A statement of partnership liquidation summarizes the above transactions, indicating the capital balances of each partner after each step in the liquidation process.

REVIEW QUESTIONS

Instructions: Analyze each of the following items carefully before writing your answer in the column at the right.

		Question	Answer
LO 1	**1.**	When two or more individuals engage in an enterprise as co-owners, the organization is known as a(n) ________.	____________
LO 1	**2.**	A written agreement containing the various provisions under which a partnership is to operate is known as a(n) ________. ..	____________
LO 1	**3.**	The characteristic of a partnership in which any partner can bind the other partners to a contract if he or she is acting within the general scope of the business is called ________.	____________
LO 1	**4.**	The characteristic of a partnership in which each general partner is personally liable for all debts incurred by the partnership is called ________.	____________
LO 1	**5.**	One of the disadvantages of the partnership form of organization is that with the death of one of the partners, the partnership ________.	____________
LO 2	**6.**	In opening the books of a partnership, a separate ________ is made for the investment of each partner.	____________
LO 2	**7.**	Each partner's capital account should be credited for the difference between the ________ invested and ________ assumed.	____________ ____________
LO 2	**8.**	When two or more sole proprietors form a partnership, their respective ________ serve as the basis for the opening entries for the investments of such partners.	____________
LO 2	**9.**	When two sole proprietors decide to combine their businesses, assets should be recorded at their ________ as of the date of formation of the partnership.	____________
LO 3	**10.**	The basis on which profits and losses are shared is a matter of agreement among the partners and not necessarily the same as their ________.	____________
LO 3	**11.**	In accounting for the operations of a partnership, it is necessary to keep a separate ________ and ________ for each partner. ...	____________ ____________
LO 3	**12.**	In the absence of any agreement among the partners, profits and losses must be shared ________, regardless of the ratio of the partners' investments.	____________

LO 3 13. Assume two partners, Beck and Call, had agreed to share profits according to a 60-40 basis, but they had no agreement on sharing losses. If there were a loss of $12,000, Call's share of the loss would be ________. .... ____________

LO 3 14. The allocation of net income and its impact on the partners' capital balances should be disclosed in the ________. .... ____________

LO 3 15. The allocation of net income is often reported in the lower portion of the ________. .... ____________

LO 4 16. The ________ section of the balance sheet should also report the equity of each partner. .... ____________

LO 5 17. ________ of a partnership may occur because of the addition of a new partner, the death or withdrawal of one of the partners, or bankruptcy. .... ____________

LO 5 18. Dissolution of the partnership does not necessarily imply that ________ will halt. .... ____________

LO 5 19. Because partnerships are dissolved under certain conditions, they are said to have ________. .... ____________

LO 5 20. By agreement, a partner may retire and be permitted to withdraw assets ________, ________, or ________ than the amount of the retiring partner's interest in the partnership. .... ____________

____

____

LO 5 21. The book value of a partner's interest is shown by the ________ of the partner's capital account. .... ____________

LO 5 22. If a retiring partner agrees to withdraw less than the amount accumulated in his or her capital account, the effect of the transaction will ________ the capital accounts of the remaining partners. .... ____________

LO 6 23. ________ of a partnership generally means that the assets are sold, liabilities are paid, and the remaining cash or other assets are distributed to the partners. .... ____________

LO 6 24. A statement of ________ summarizes the transactions involved in liquidating a partnership. .... ____________

EXERCISES

Exercise 1 (LO 2) PARTNERSHIP OPENING ENTRIES

On June 1, 20--, Mary Campbell and Barb Stanley agreed to form a partnership to market firewood. They agreed to invest $20,000 and $25,000, respectively. Prepare the opening entries for the cash investments.

GENERAL JOURNAL PAGE

	DATE	DESCRIPTION	POST. REF.	DEBIT	CREDIT	
1						1
2						2
3						3
4						4
5						5
6						6
7						7
8						8
9						9
10						10
11						11
12						12
13						13
14						14
15						15

Exercise 2 (LO 2) PARTNERSHIP OPENING ENTRIES

Jim Hassel and Mark Back currently own and operate independent shoe stores on opposite sides of town. On January 1, 20-2, they decided to form a partnership, Hassel & Back Shoes, by combining their businesses. Post-closing trial balances for each firm on December 31, 20-1, are provided below.

Hassel Shoes
Post-Closing Trial Balance
December 31, 20-1

Cash	$ 3,300	
Merchandise Inventory	38,000	
Store Equipment	28,000	
Accumulated Depreciation—Store Equipment		$ 8,000
Notes Payable		20,000
Accounts Payable		15,000
Jim Hassel, Capital		26,300
	$69,300	$69,300

Exercise 2 (Concluded)

Back Shoes
Post-Closing Trial Balance
December 31, 20-1

Cash	$12,100	
Merchandise Inventory	24,000	
Notes Payable		$ 5,000
Accounts Payable		8,000
Mark Back, Capital		23,100
	$36,100	$36,100

Hassel and Back agree that since both have been using the FIFO method of valuing inventory, these amounts approximate fair market values. The fair market value of the store equipment is $25,000.

Prepare the opening entries for the investments of Hassel and Back.

GENERAL JOURNAL

PAGE

	DATE	DESCRIPTION	POST. REF.	DEBIT	CREDIT	
1						1
2						2
3						3
4						4
5						5
6						6
7						7
8						8
9						9
10						10
11						11
12						12
13						13
14						14
15						15

Exercise 3 (LO 4) PARTIAL FINANCIAL STATEMENT

Fisher and Worth have been partners in the book business for several years and have shared profits on a 60-40 basis. Capital balances on January 1 were $85,000 and $64,000, respectively. No additional investments were made during the year, and withdrawals were $35,000 and $28,000, respectively. Net income for the year was $78,000. Prepare the statement of partners' equity and the partners' equity section of the balance sheet for the partnership as of December 31, 20--.

Exercise 4 (LO 5) ADMITTING NEW PARTNERS

Chuck Green and Mary Yellow have been operating a successful paint store for several years. On July 30, 20-4, Susan Blue was admitted as a new partner for a cash investment of $60,000. Blue was given a capital interest equal to her cash investment. Prepare the journal entry to admit Blue to the partnership.

GENERAL JOURNAL

PAGE

	DATE		DESCRIPTION	POST. REF.	DEBIT	CREDIT	
1							1
2							2
3							3
4							4
5							5

Exercise 5 (LO 5) ADMITTING A NEW PARTNER

Bill Dodd and Nancy Kirk are partners in a construction business. On May 16, 20-3, they admitted Linda Philipich as a new partner. Linda has operated her own construction business for several years and has the following assets and liabilities that will be contributed to the new partnership:

Philipich Construction
Post-Closing Trial Balance
May 16, 20-3

Cash	$ 8,300	
Accounts Receivable	12,000	
Allowance for Bad Debts		$ 2,000
Construction Equipment	48,000	
Accum. Depreciation—Construction Equip.		18,000
Notes Payable		15,000
Accounts Payable		5,000
Linda Philipich, Capital		28,300
	$68,300	$68,300

Philipich has no knowledge of specific uncollectible accounts receivable, and the construction equipment is valued at $35,000. No bonus was received or granted. Prepare the journal entry to admit Philipich as a new partner.

GENERAL JOURNAL PAGE

	DATE		DESCRIPTION	POST. REF.	DEBIT	CREDIT	
1							1
2							2
3							3
4							4
5							5
6							6
7							7
8							8
9							9

Exercise 6 (LO 5) WITHDRAWAL OF A PARTNER

Write, Beck, and Campbell have operated the Quick Stop Food Mart as a partnership for many years. The partners have agreed that on December 31, 20-6, Campbell will retire from the business and withdraw cash equivalent to the balance in his capital account. Capital balances for each partner are listed below.

J. B. Write, Capital	$84,200
L. L. Beck, Capital	92,800
R. W. Campbell, Capital	78,000

Prepare the journal entry for the withdrawal of Campbell.

Exercise 6 (LO 5) (Concluded)

GENERAL JOURNAL PAGE

	DATE		DESCRIPTION	POST. REF.	DEBIT	CREDIT	
1							1
2							2
3							3
4							4
5							5

Exercise 7 (LO 6) PARTNERSHIP LIQUIDATION

On liquidation of the partnership of L. Ling and S. Salk, as of October 1, 20--, inventory with a book value of $92,000 is sold for $101,000. Considering that Ling and Salk share profits and losses equally, prepare the entries for the sale and the allocation of gain.

GENERAL JOURNAL PAGE

	DATE		DESCRIPTION	POST. REF.	DEBIT	CREDIT	
1							1
2							2
3							3
4							4
5							5
6							6
7							7
8							8
9							9
10							10
11							11
12							12
13							13
14							14
15							15

PROBLEMS

Problem 8 (LO 2) PARTNERSHIP OPENING ENTRIES

Fred Dusk and Nancy Dawn have been sole proprietors of separate drive-in theaters for several years. On January 1, 20-4, they form a partnership called Dusk to Dawn Drive-In Theaters. The following balance sheets provided for each business serve as the basis for the partnership:

Fred Dusk
Balance Sheet
December 31, 20-3

Assets		
Cash		$ 3,200
Accounts receivable	$ 2,524	
Less allowance for bad debts	430	2,094
Merchandise inventory		4,800
Projection equipment	$ 9,900	
Less accumulated depreciation	1,000	8,900
Snack bar and facilities	$25,000	
Less accumulated depreciation	5,500	19,500
Total assets		$38,494
Liabilities		
Notes payable	$13,500	
Accounts payable	5,480	
Total liabilities		$18,980
Owner's Equity		
Fred Dusk, capital		19,514
Total liabilities and owner's equity		$38,494

Nancy Dawn
Balance Sheet
December 31, 20-3

Assets		
Cash		$ 1,533
Accounts receivable	$ 2,160	
Less allowance for bad debts	320	1,840
Merchandise inventory		11,400
Supplies		356
Office equipment	$ 6,220	
Less accumulated depreciation	1,100	5,120
Projection equipment	$14,800	
Less accumulated depreciation	2,200	12,600
Snack bar and facilities	$52,500	
Less accumulated depreciation	6,000	46,500
Total assets		$79,349
Liabilities		
Notes payable	$26,000	
Accounts payable	16,300	
Total liabilities		$42,300
Owner's Equity		
Nancy Dawn, capital		37,049
Total liabilities and owner's equity		$79,349

Problem 8 (Concluded)

Dusk and Dawn agree that the information provided on the balance sheets represents market values, except for the assets listed below for which appraisals of current market values were obtained. Neither Dusk nor Dawn has any knowledge of uncollectible accounts.

	Appraised Market Values	
	Dusk	Dawn
Office equipment		$ 4,800
Projection equipment	$ 7,500	11,200
Snack bar and facilities	18,500	48,000

Required:

Prepare opening entries for the investments of Dusk and Dawn.

GENERAL JOURNAL PAGE

DATE	DESCRIPTION	POST. REF.	DEBIT	CREDIT

Problem 9 (LO 3/4) ALLOCATION OF NET INCOME, PREPARATION OF FINANCIAL STATEMENTS AND CLOSING ENTRIES

Refer to Problem 8. The partnership agreement between Dusk and Dawn calls for yearly salary allowances for Dusk and Dawn of $35,000 and $45,000, respectively.

Further, each partner is to receive 12% interest on his/her capital balances as of January 1. The remaining income or loss is allocated 40% to Dusk and 60% to Dawn. During 20-4, net income amounted to $176,500; Dusk made an additional investment of $10,000 on July 6; and each partner withdrew an amount equal to his/her annual salary.

Required:

1. Prepare the lower portion of the income statement for Dusk to Dawn Drive-In Theaters reporting the allocation of net income (round to nearest dollar).
2. Prepare a statement of partners' equity for the year ended December 31, 20-4.
3. Prepare the partners' equity section of the balance sheet.
4. Prepare entries to close Income Summary and each partner's drawing account.

1.

2.

Problem 9 (Concluded)

3.

4.

GENERAL JOURNAL PAGE

	DATE		DESCRIPTION	POST. REF.	DEBIT	CREDIT	
1							1
2							2
3							3
4							4
5							5
6							6
7							7
8							8
9							9
10							10
11							11

Problem 10 (LO 5) ADMITTING A NEW PARTNER

Kelmski and Saliman are partners in the K & S Music Store. Bob Murry who has owned and operated Murry's Music Store for many years will join the partnership of Kelmski and Saliman. The balance sheet for Murry's as of May 31, 20-1, is provided below.

Murry's Music Store
Balance Sheet
May 31, 20-1

Assets		
Cash		$ 3,200
Accounts receivable	$22,524	
Less allowance for bad debts	1,200	21,324
Merchandise inventory		84,800
Office equipment	$ 8,500	
Less accumulated depreciation	1,000	7,500
Total assets		$116,824
Liabilities		
Notes payable	$12,200	
Accounts payable	25,480	
Total liabilities		$ 37,680
Owner's Equity		
Bob Murry, capital		79,144
Total liabilities and owner's equity		$116,824

The values reported on the balance sheet are reasonable approximations for market, except for the office equipment that is valued at $5,000. Murry has no knowledge of any uncollectible accounts receivable.

Required:

Prepare the journal entry for the admittance of Murry as a new partner on June 1, 20-1.

GENERAL JOURNAL PAGE

	DATE	DESCRIPTION	POST. REF.	DEBIT	CREDIT	
1						1
2						2
3						3
4						4
5						5
6						6
7						7
8						8
9						9
10						10

Problem 11 (LO 5) WITHDRAWAL OF A PARTNER

Casler, Courtney, and Snavely have been partners in a recycling business for several years. On May 1, 20-5, Courtney withdrew from the partnership with the agreement that the partnership would pay $26,000 cash for his share of the business. According to the partnership agreement, any difference between the amount paid to a withdrawing partner and the book value of the partner's capital account is allocated to the remaining partners according to the ratio of their capital interests. The capital balances for the partners on May 1, 20-5, after allocating net income and closing their drawing accounts, are as follows:

S. S. Casler, Capital	$45,000
J. D. Courtney, Capital	30,000
E. R. Snavely, Capital	15,000

Required:

1. Prepare the journal entry for the withdrawal of Courtney.

GENERAL JOURNAL PAGE

	DATE	DESCRIPTION	POST. REF.	DEBIT	CREDIT	
1						1
2						2
3						3
4						4
5						5
6						6
7						7

2. Instead of the foregoing, assume the partnership paid $38,000 for Courtney's share of the business. Prepare the journal entry for the withdrawal of Courtney.

GENERAL JOURNAL PAGE

	DATE	DESCRIPTION	POST. REF.	DEBIT	CREDIT	
1						1
2						2
3						3
4						4
5						5
6						6
7						7

Problem 11 (Concluded)

3. Instead of the foregoing, assume Snavely paid Courtney $40,000 for his share of the business. Prepare the journal entry required in the partnership's books for the withdrawal of Courtney.

GENERAL JOURNAL PAGE

	DATE		DESCRIPTION	POST. REF.	DEBIT	CREDIT	
1							1
2							2
3							3
4							4
5							5
6							6
7							7

Problem 12 (LO 6) STATEMENT OF PARTNERSHIP LIQUIDATION

After many years of operations, the partnership of Thay, Walter, and Carpenter is to be liquidated. The June 30, 20--, post-closing trial balance for the partnership is provided below.

Thay, Walter, and Carpenter
Post-Closing Trial Balance
June 30, 20--

	Account Balance	
Account Title	Debit	Credit
Cash	$ 18,300	
Inventory	28,000	
Other Assets	75,000	
Liabilities		$ 13,000
G. B. Thay, Capital		35,200
E. F. Walter, Capital		39,900
Q. E. Carpenter, Capital		33,200
	$121,300	$121,300

Profits and losses are shared equally.

Required:

1. Prepare a statement of partnership liquidation for the period July 1–7, 20--.
   a. The sale of noncash assets on July 1 for $94,000.
   b. The allocation of any gain or loss to the partners on July 1.
   c. The payment of liabilities on July 3.
   d. The distribution of cash to the partners on July 7.
2. Journalize these four transactions in a general journal.

Problem 12 (Continued)

1.

Thay, Walter, and Carpenter
Statement of Partnership Liquidation
For period July 1–7, 20--

			Other		Capital		
	Cash	Inventory	Assets	Liabilities	Thay	Walter	Carpenter
Balance before sale of assets							
Sale of noncash assets and alloc. of loss							
Balance after sale							
Payment of liabilities							
Balance after payment of liabilities							
Distribution of cash to partners							
Final balances							

Problem 12 (Concluded)

2.

GENERAL JOURNAL PAGE

	DATE		DESCRIPTION	POST. REF.	DEBIT	CREDIT	
1							1
2							2
3							3
4							4
5							5
6							6
7							7
8							8
9							9
10							10
11							11
12							12
13							13
14							14
15							15
16							16
17							17
18							18
19							19
20							20
21							21
22							22

CHAPTER 20
CORPORATIONS: ORGANIZATION AND CAPITAL STOCK

LEARNING OBJECTIVES

Chapter 20 describes the corporation—its organization and characteristics, types of capital stock, capital stock transactions, and the stockholders' equity section of the balance sheet.

Objective 1. Describe the characteristics, formation, and organization of a corporation.

A **corporation** is a legal entity that exists separate from its owners. It is taxed on its income and is subject to government regulations that do not apply to partnerships and proprietorships. Yet the corporation offers many significant advantages—limited liability of its owners, transferability of ownership interests (**shares** of stock), ease of raising capital (selling stock), limited powers of owners, and unlimited life (the corporation goes on even when owners die or leave the business).

When a corporation is formed, a **charter**, or **articles of incorporation**, is prepared. **Stockholders** are owners of shares of stock in the corporation; stockholders elect a **board of directors** that determines policy and hires officers. **Organization costs** (attorneys' fees, incorporation fees, promotion expenses) are expensed when incurred.

Objective 2. Describe stockholders' equity and the types of capital stock, and compute dividends on preferred and common stock.

In a corporation, owners' equity is called **stockholders' equity**. **Paid-in capital** is the amount stockholders paid for shares of stock; **retained earnings** is accumulated earnings that have not been paid out to stockholders in the form of **dividends**.

Capital stock may be ***par value, no-par,*** or ***stated value*** stock. It may also be ***common stock*** or ***preferred stock*** that has certain preferences or superior rights. For example, the owners of **preferred stock** usually have the right to receive dividends of a certain amount before the owners of **common stock** can receive any. In addition, **cumulative preferred stock** has a carryover right for dividends unpaid in a given year. This means that dividends for the unpaid year are distributed to preferred stockholders before common stockholders receive dividends.

Objective 3. Account for capital stock transactions.

Stock may be issued at *par or above par* (at a **premium**). ***No-par stock*** does not carry a specified value, and no premium is involved. Stock with a **stated value** is treated the same as stock with **par value**.

Stock may be issued for either cash or noncash assets. Noncash assets are recorded at the fair **market value** of the assets or of the stock, whichever can be more clearly determined.

Capital stock subscriptions are agreements whereby a **subscriber** agrees to purchase shares of stock at a specified price. A receivable is created; and when the shares are paid for in full, stock is issued. If there is a difference between the amount receivable and the par or stated value of the stock, the difference is credited to Paid-In Capital in Excess of Par on Common (or Preferred) Stock.

Treasury stock is stock reacquired by the corporation. Treasury stock may be resold, but no gain or loss is recognized. Any difference between the price for reacquiring the stock and the price for reselling it is debited or credited to Paid-In Capital from Sale of Treasury Stock.

Objective 4. Prepare the stockholders' equity section of a corporation balance sheet.

The stockholders' equity section of a corporate balance sheet is quite different from a proprietorship or partnership balance sheet. Common and preferred stocks issued are listed, together with subscriptions, paid-in capital in excess of par and from sale of treasury stock, and retained earnings. Stock subscriptions receivable and treasury stock are deducted from the total of the paid-in capital and retained earnings.

REVIEW QUESTIONS

Instructions: Analyze each of the following items carefully before writing your answer in the column at the right.

	Question	Answer
LO 1	**1.** Limited ________ means that owners do not have personal liability for the debts of the corporation.	________________
LO 1	**2.** The owners' equity in a corporation is called ________.	________________
LO 1	**3.** Capital stock is divided into ________, which represent ownership rights in the corporation.	________________
LO 1	**4.** ________ means that each owner has the power to act as an agent and engage in contracts for the business.	________________
LO 1	**5.** Unlike partnerships and proprietorships, corporations must pay ________ taxes.	________________
LO 1	**6.** Distributions of corporate income to its owners are called ______.	________________
LO 1	**7.** A(n) ________ or articles of incorporation is a legal document that forms a corporation.	________________
LO 1	**8.** The incorporators elect a temporary board of directors to prepare the ________, which, together with the charter, provide guidelines for the business.	________________
LO 1	**9.** Owners of capital stock of a corporation are called ________. ..	________________
LO 1	**10.** A permanent ________ is elected by the stockholders and sets policies and selects officers.	________________
LO 1	**11.** Costs of organizing a corporation such as attorneys' fees are called ________.	________________
LO 2	**12.** The amount paid by stockholders for their shares of stock is called ________.	________________
LO 2	**13.** ________ is the corporation's accumulated earnings that have not been paid out in dividends.	________________
LO 2	**14.** The total number of shares of stock a corporation is allowed to sell is called ________ stock.	________________
LO 2	**15.** Capital stock that has been sold is called ________ stock.	________________
LO 2	**16.** Stock that has been reacquired by a corporation is called _______ stock.	________________
LO 2	**17.** Issued stock less treasury stock equals ________ stock, the shares in the hands of the stockholders.	________________
LO 2	**18.** Shares that have a dollar amount per share printed on the certificate are called ________ stocks.	________________

LO 2 19. ________ value is the amount at which stock can be sold on the open market. .... ____________

LO 2 20. Stock that has no dollar amount printed on it is called ________ stock. .... ____________

LO 2 21. Stock that is assigned a value per share by the board of directors is called ________ stock. .... ____________

LO 2 22. Stock that gives its owners the right to vote at stockholders' meetings is called ________ stock. .... ____________

LO 2 23. ________ stock has certain privileges or rights that are superior but typically has no voting rights. .... ____________

LO 2 24. Preferred stock that has claims for dividends that accumulate from year to year is called ________ stock. .... ____________

LO 3 25. When par value stock is issued at a price above par, the amount above par is called a(n) ________. .... ____________

LO 3 26. A capital stock ________ is an agreement to buy shares of stock at a specific price. .... ____________

LO 4 27. In the stockholders' equity section of the balance sheet, ________ stock is listed first. .... ____________

EXERCISES

Exercise 1 (LO 1) ACCOUNTING FOR ORGANIZATION COSTS

Prepare a journal entry to record payment of the following organization costs incurred by Duncan Donuts:

Incorporation fees	$ 900
Attorneys' fees	5,000
Promotion expenses	3,100

GENERAL JOURNAL PAGE

	DATE		DESCRIPTION	POST. REF.	DEBIT	CREDIT	
1							1
2							2
3							3
4							4
5							5
6							6
7							7
8							8

Exercise 2 (LO 2) DIVIDEND ALLOCATIONS

Prepare the dividend allocation of J. L. Adams Company, which has the following stock outstanding:

Common Stock	Preferred Stock
10,000 shares	5,000 shares
$5 par value	$8 dividend, $50 par

The amount available for dividends this year is $50,000.

Exercise 3 (LO 2) DIVIDEND ALLOCATIONS

Prepare the dividend allocation for M. B. Oliver Company, which has the following stock outstanding:

Common Stock	Preferred Stock
25,000 shares	Cumulative: 4,000 shares
$8 par value	$25 par, $4 dividend
	Noncumulative: 6,000 shares
	$20 par, $3 dividend

The amount available for dividends this year is $113,000. No dividends were paid last year.

Exercise 4 (LO 4) STOCKHOLDERS' EQUITY SECTION

Prepare the stockholders' equity section of the balance sheet for PrimeCorp Products as of December 31, 20--. After closing its books, stockholders' equity accounts have the following balances:

Common stock subscriptions receivable	$14,000
Common stock, $4 par, 14,000 shares	56,000
Preferred stock, $12 par, 8%, 6,000 shares	72,000
Common stock subscribed, $4 par, 12,000 shares	48,000
Retained earnings	33,000

PROBLEMS

Problem 5 (LO 3) PAR AND NO-PAR, COMMON AND PREFERRED STOCK

Required:

Prepare journal entries for the following stock transactions. Using a general journal, label the entries (a) through (h).

(a) Issued 10,000 shares of $4 par common stock for $40,000 cash.
(b) Issued 4,000 shares of $4 par common stock for $17,200 cash.
(c) Issued 3,000 shares of $10 par, 8% preferred stock for $32,000 cash.
(d) Issued 3,300 shares of no-par common stock for $15,000.
(e) Issued 6,000 shares of no-par common stock with a stated value of $5 per share for $30,000 cash.
(f) Issued 4,800 shares of no-par common stock with a stated value of $5 per share for $25,500 cash.
(g) Issued 10,000 shares of $5 par common stock for land with a fair market value of $50,000.
(h) Issued 8,000 shares of $5 par common stock for a truck with a fair market value of $41,500.

GENERAL JOURNAL

PAGE

	DATE	DESCRIPTION	POST. REF.	DEBIT	CREDIT	
1						1
2						2
3						3
4						4
5						5
6						6
7						7
8						8
9						9
10						10
11						11
12						12
13						13
14						14
15						15
16						16
17						17
18						18
19						19
20						20
21						21

Problem 5 (Concluded)

GENERAL JOURNAL

PAGE

	DATE		DESCRIPTION	POST. REF.	DEBIT	CREDIT	
1							1
2							2
3							3
4							4
5							5
6							6
7							7
8							8
9							9
10							10
11							11
12							12
13							13
14							14
15							15
16							16
17							17
18							18
19							19
20							20
21							21
22							22
23							23
24							24
25							25
26							26
27							27
28							28
29							29
30							30
31							31
32							32
33							33
34							34

Problem 6 (LO 3) STOCK SUBSCRIPTIONS

Required:

Prepare journal entries for the following stock transactions. Using a general journal, label the entries (a) through (i).

(a) Received subscriptions for 4,000 shares of $8 par common stock for $32,000. (J. K. Adams)
(b) Received subscriptions for 3,800 shares of $7 par common stock for $27,000. (R. L. Jones)
(c) Received $16,000 cash from J. K. Adams on the common stock subscription in (a).
(d) Received subscriptions for 5,000 shares of 8%, $13 par preferred stock for $66,000. (T. K. Lyman)
(e) Received $13,500 cash from R. L. Jones on the common stock subscription in (b).
(f) Received $33,000 cash from T. K. Lyman on the preferred stock subscription in (d).
(g) Received balance in full from J. K. Adams for the common stock subscription in (a) and (c). (Stock is issued.)
(h) Received balance in full from R. L. Jones for the common stock subscription in (b) and (e). (Stock is issued.)
(i) Received balance in full from T. K. Lyman for the preferred stock subscription in (d) and (f). (Stock is issued.)

GENERAL JOURNAL

PAGE

	DATE	DESCRIPTION	POST. REF.	DEBIT	CREDIT	
1						1
2						2
3						3
4						4
5						5
6						6
7						7
8						8
9						9
10						10
11						11
12						12
13						13
14						14
15						15
16						16
17						17

Problem 6 (Continued)

GENERAL JOURNAL

PAGE

DATE		DESCRIPTION	POST. REF.	DEBIT	CREDIT

Name ______________________________

Problem 6 (Concluded)

GENERAL JOURNAL

PAGE

DATE	DESCRIPTION	POST. REF.	DEBIT	CREDIT

Problem 7 (LO 1/3) ORGANIZATION COSTS, STOCK SUBSCRIPTIONS, AND TREASURY STOCK

Required:

Based on the following information, prepare general journal entries. Label the entries by date.

Mar.	28	Incurred the following costs of incorporation: Incorporation fees $ 900 Attorneys' fees 6,000 Promotion fees 5,700
Apr.	12	Issued 10,000 shares of $8 par common stock for $81,200.
May	1	Received subscriptions for 4,000 shares of $8 par common stock for $32,500.
June	21	Received a payment of $16,500 cash for the common stock subscription.
July	5	Purchased 1,000 shares of its own $8 par common stock for $9 a share.
	12	Issued 4,000 shares of no-par common stock with a stated value of $7 for $28,200.
Aug.	21	Received the balance in full for the common stock subscription. Issued the stock.
Sept.	28	Sold 500 shares of treasury stock for $9.50 a share.
Nov.	9	Issued 5,000 shares of 9%, $15 par value preferred stock in exchange for land with a fair market value of $75,600.
Dec.	20	Sold 500 shares of treasury stock for $8.75 a share.

GENERAL JOURNAL

PAGE

DATE		DESCRIPTION	POST. REF.	DEBIT	CREDIT

Problem 7 (Concluded)

GENERAL JOURNAL

PAGE

DATE		DESCRIPTION	POST. REF.	DEBIT	CREDIT

Problem 8 (LO 4) STOCKHOLDERS' EQUITY SECTION

After closing its books on December 31, 20--, Landry Company's stockholders' equity accounts have the following balances:

Account	Balance	Additional Information
Preferred Stock Subscriptions Receivable	$ 15,000	
Common Stock Subscriptions Receivable	25,000	
Preferred Stock, 8%	100,000	$10 par, 10,000 shares
Common Stock	250,000	$5 par, 50,000 shares
Preferred Stock Subscribed, 8%	50,000	$10 par, 5,000 shares
Common Stock Subscribed	100,000	$5 par, 20,000 shares
Paid-In Capital in Excess of Par—Preferred Stock	18,000	
Paid-In Capital from Sale of Treasury Stock	9,000	
Retained Earnings	62,000	
Common Treasury Stock	20,000	

Required:
Prepare the stockholders' equity section of the balance sheet.

CHAPTER 21
CORPORATIONS: TAXES, EARNINGS, DISTRIBUTIONS, AND THE STATEMENT OF RETAINED EARNINGS

LEARNING OBJECTIVES

Chapter 21 continues the discussion of stockholders' equity for a corporate form of business. This chapter is concerned with transactions that affect retained earnings.

Objective 1. Account for corporate income taxes.

Corporations must pay income taxes based on their earnings. Sole proprietorships and partnerships, as businesses, do not pay income taxes. Most corporations must estimate their annual income taxes and make quarterly payments. At the end of the year, an adjusting entry is typically necessary to recognize the correct amount of income taxes for the year.

Objective 2. Explain the use of the retained earnings account.

Typically, the only credit to the retained earnings account is for the net income of a period. The only debits are for a net loss, closing the dividends account, and appropriations of retained earnings.

The adjusting and closing process at the end of the period is virtually the same for corporations as for sole proprietorships and partnerships. One difference for corporations is that after all revenues and expenses are closed to Income Summary, net income is transferred into the retained earnings account with the following entry:

Income Summary	xx	
Retained Earnings		xx

A net loss is transferred into the retained earnings account with the following entry:

Retained Earnings	xx	
Income Summary		xx

In addition, the dividends account is closed to Retained Earnings with the following entry:

Retained Earnings	xx	
Dividends		xx

Objective 3. Account for dividends and stock splits.

A distribution of earnings by a corporation to its stockholders is known as a **dividend.**

A dividend payable in cash is known as a **cash dividend**. For a corporation to issue a cash dividend, the following three conditions are necessary:

1. Unrestricted retained earnings
2. Adequate cash balance
3. Declaration of dividend

Three dates are involved in the declaration and payment of dividends.

1. **Date of declaration**
2. **Date of record**
3. **Date of payment**

Of the above dates, only the date of declaration and date of payment require entries in the general journal.

Declaration of a cash dividend is accounted for as follows:

Cash Dividends	XX	
Preferred or Common Dividends Payable		XX

Payment of a cash dividend is accounted for as follows:

Preferred or Common Dividends Payable	XX	
Cash		XX

A **stock dividend** is a proportionate distribution of shares of a corporation's own stock to its stockholders. **Stock dividends** typically are stated as a percentage of common stock outstanding. For stock dividends of less than 20–25%, Retained Earnings is debited for the market value of the stock. Either the par or stated value is used to credit Stock Dividends Distributable. The excess of the market value over par or stated value is credited to Paid-In Capital. If the stock has neither par nor stated value, Stock Dividends Distributable is credited for the market value of the shares.

The journal entry for the declaration of a stock dividend is as follows:

Stock Dividends	XX	
Stock Dividends Distributable		XX
Paid-In Capital in Excess of Par or Stated Value		XX

The journal entry for the distribution of a stock dividend is as follows:

Stock Dividends Distributable	XX	
Common Stock		XX

For stock dividends of more than 20–25%, Stock Dividends is debited for the par or stated value of the stock. Stock dividends do not affect the assets, liabilities, or stockholders' equity of the corporation. Stock dividends merely transfer part of the balance of the retained earnings account to one or more paid-in capital accounts.

A **stock split** is an exchange of one share of an old issue of stock for a multiple number of shares of a new issue with a reduced par or stated value. The usual purpose of a stock split is to improve the marketability of the shares by reducing the market price per share. No formal journal entry is made for a stock split.

Objective 4. Account for restriction of retained earnings.

A **retained earnings appropriation** is a restriction of retained earnings by the board of directors for a specific purpose. A retained earnings appropriation is used primarily to limit the availability of retained earnings for paying dividends.

The journal entry to account for an appropriation of retained earnings is as follows:

Retained Earnings	XX	
Retained Earnings Appropriated for (*specific purpose*)		XX

After the retained earnings appropriation has served its purpose, the appropriated amount can be returned to retained earnings. The journal entry showing this is as follows:

Retained Earnings Appropriated for (*specific purpose*)	XX	
Retained Earnings		XX

The practice of appropriating retained earnings is unusual today. Restriction of retained earnings often can be described more clearly in a footnote to the financial statements.

Objective 5. Prepare a statement of retained earnings.

A **statement of retained earnings** explains the change in the amount of retained earnings during the year. All of the information necessary to prepare the statement of retained earnings is contained in the unappropriated and appropriated retained earnings accounts in the general ledger. If there are both appropriated and unappropriated retained earnings, each is shown separately in the statement of retained earnings.

REVIEW QUESTIONS

Instructions: Analyze each of the following items carefully before writing your answer in the column at the right.

		Question	Answer
LO 1	**1.**	When corporate income taxes are estimated for the year, quarterly payments are made. The account title debited for each of these payments is ________.	________________
LO 2	**2.**	Name the two major sources of capital for every type of business.	________________ ________________
LO 2	**3.**	Typically, the only credit to Retained Earnings is for the ______ of a period.	________________
LO 2	**4.**	Typically, the only debits to Retained Earnings are for _______, ________, and ________.	________________ ________________ ________________
LO 2	**5.**	A credit balance in the income summary account represents ________ for the period.	________________
LO 2	**6.**	If there is a net loss for the accounting period, the closing of the net loss involves a debit to _______ and a credit to _______.	________________ ________________
LO 3	**7.**	A distribution of earnings by a corporation to its stockholders is known as a(n) ________.	________________
LO 3	**8.**	The two types of dividends are a(n) ________ dividend and a(n) ________ dividend.	________________ ________________
LO 3	**9.**	Name the three conditions necessary for a corporation to issue a cash dividend.	________________ ________________ ________________
LO 3	**10.**	The date on which the board of directors decides or declares that a dividend is to be paid is called the ________.	________________
LO 3	**11.**	The date on which the names of stockholders entitled to receive the dividend are determined is called the ________.	________________
LO 3	**12.**	The date on which the dividend is actually paid by the corporation is called the ________.	________________
LO 3	**13.**	The account title debited when a cash dividend on common stock is declared is the ________ account.	________________
LO 3	**14.**	The account title debited when a cash dividend on common stock is paid is the ________ account.	________________

LO 3 15. On the balance sheet, Dividends Payable is classified as a(n) ________. .... ________________

LO 3 16. A proportionate distribution of shares of a corporation's own stock to its stockholders is called a(n) ________. .... ________________

LO 3 17. When journalizing the declaration of a stock dividend on common stock, the account title ________ is credited for the par or stated value of the stock. .... ________________

LO 3 18. When journalizing the distribution of a stock dividend declared on common stock, the account title ________ is debited and the account title ________ is credited. .... ________________

____

LO 3 19. A stock dividend merely transfers part of the balance of the ________ account to one or more ________ accounts. .... ________________

____

LO 3 20. An exchange of one share of an old issue of stock for a multiple number of shares of a new issue with a reduced par or stated value is known as a(n) ________. .... ________________

LO 3 21. A stock split requires no formal journal entry and may be recognized simply by a(n) ________ in the general journal. .... ________________

LO 4 22. A(n) ________ is a restriction of retained earnings by the board of directors for a specific purpose. .... ________________

LO 5 23. A(n) ________ explains the change in the amount of retained earnings during the year. .... ________________

LO 5 24. All of the information necessary to prepare the statement of retained earnings is contained in the ________ and ________ retained earnings accounts in the general ledger. .... ________________

____

EXERCISES

Exercise 1 (LO 1) CORPORATE INCOME TAX

Chamberlain Company estimates that its 20-1 income tax will be $100,000. Based on this estimate, it will make four quarterly payments of $25,000 each April 15, June 15, September 15, and December 15.

1. Prepare the journal entry for April 15.
2. Assume all four quarterly payments have been entered in the general journal. On December 31, Chamberlain Company's actual income tax amounts to $107,000, and the balance is due and payable on March 15, 20-2. Prepare the journal entry to record the additional income tax owed.

Exercise 1 (Concluded)

GENERAL JOURNAL PAGE

	DATE		DESCRIPTION	POST. REF.	DEBIT	CREDIT	
1							1
2							2
3							3
4							4
5							5
6							6
7							7
8							8
9							9
10							10
11							11
12							12
13							13
14							14
15							15

Exercise 2 (LO 2/4) INCOME SUMMARY, DIVIDENDS, AND RETAINED EARNINGS

Prepare appropriate general journal entries for the following events affecting the retained earnings accounts of Hylan Co. and Lolan Co. Then answer the questions that follow.

Dec.	31	Hylan's income summary account credit balance of $72,100 is closed.
	31	Hylan's cash dividends account debit balance of $23,000 is closed.
	31	Lolan's income summary account debit balance of $38,000 is closed.
	31	Lolan's stock dividends account debit balance of $15,000 is closed.
	31	Lolan's board of directors appropriated $20,000 of retained earnings for bond interest.

Exercise 2 (Concluded)

GENERAL JOURNAL

PAGE

	DATE		DESCRIPTION	POST. REF.	DEBIT	CREDIT	
1							1
2							2
3							3
4							4
5							5
6							6
7							7
8							8
9							9
10							10
11							11
12							12
13							13
14							14
15							15

1. What did the credit balance in Hylan's income summary account represent?
2. What did the debit balance in Hylan's cash dividends account represent?
3. What did the debit balance in Lolan's income summary account represent?
4. What did the debit balance in Lolan's stock dividends account represent?

Exercise 3 (LO 3) COMMON CASH DIVIDENDS

Prepare general journal entries for the declaration and payment of a cash dividend on common stock for Davis Company.

Sept.	3	Declared a cash dividend of $2 per share to common shareholders of record, September 30, payable on October 5. Davis Company has 50,000 shares of $5 par value common stock outstanding.
Oct.	5	Paid the cash dividend.

GENERAL JOURNAL PAGE

	DATE		DESCRIPTION	POST. REF.	DEBIT	CREDIT	
1							1
2							2
3							3
4							4
5							5
6							6
7							7
8							8
9							9

Exercise 4 (LO 3) PREFERRED CASH DIVIDENDS

Prepare appropriate general journal entries for each of the following transactions of Roxton Co.:

June	1	Declared a dividend of $2 per share on 8,000 shares of preferred stock outstanding.
	20	Paid the dividend on preferred stock declared on June 1.

GENERAL JOURNAL PAGE

	DATE		DESCRIPTION	POST. REF.	DEBIT	CREDIT	
1							1
2							2
3							3
4							4
5							5
6							6
7							7
8							8
9							9
10							10

Exercise 5 (LO 3) STOCK DIVIDENDS AND SPLITS

Prepare appropriate general journal entries and memo notations, as needed, for each of the following transactions of Rockmaney Co.:

Feb.	3	Declared a 15% stock dividend to common shareholders. The market value of the common stock is \$14 per share. The par value is \$10. There are 80,000 shares of common stock outstanding.
	24	Issued 12,000 shares of common stock in settlement of the stock dividend declared on February 3.
July	1	Declared a 2-for-1 stock split.

GENERAL JOURNAL PAGE

DATE	DESCRIPTION	POST. REF.	DEBIT	CREDIT

Exercise 6 (LO 5) STATEMENT OF RETAINED EARNINGS

Based on the following information, prepare a statement of retained earnings for Register Co. for the year ended December 31, 20-1.

(a) The Retained Earnings balance increased from \$80,000 on January 1 to \$119,000 on December 31.
(b) Net income for the year was \$89,000.
(c) Cash dividends of \$50,000 were paid to common stockholders.

Exercise 6 (Concluded)

PROBLEMS

Problem 7 (LO 3/4) CASH DIVIDENDS, STOCK DIVIDENDS, AND APPROPRIATION OF RETAINED EARNINGS

During the year ended December 31, 20-2, King Company completed the following selected transactions:

Mar.	20	Declared a semiannual dividend of $0.30 per share on preferred stock and $0.15 per share on common stock to shareholders of record on April 10, payable on April 15. Currently, there are 8,000 shares of $50 par value preferred stock and 90,000 shares of $5 par value common stock outstanding.
Apr.	15	Paid the preferred and common cash dividends.
June	16	King's board of directors appropriated $210,000 for the purchase of a treatment plant.
Oct.	10	Declared semiannual dividend of $0.30 per share on preferred stock and $0.15 per share on common stock to shareholders of record on November 5, payable on November 10.
Nov.	10	Paid the preferred and common cash dividends.
	17	A 10% stock dividend was declared to common shareholders of record on December 8, distributable on December 15. Market value of the common stock was estimated at $12 per share.
Dec.	15	Issued certificates for common stock dividend.
	31	Net income for 20-2 was $195,000. The income summary account is closed.
	31	The cash and stock dividends accounts are closed.

Required:

Prepare journal entries for the above transactions.

Problem 7 (Concluded)

GENERAL JOURNAL

PAGE

DATE		DESCRIPTION	POST. REF.	DEBIT	CREDIT

Problem 8 (LO 5) STATEMENT OF RETAINED EARNINGS

On January 1, 20-2, Lloyd Corporation's retained earnings accounts had the following balances:

Appropriated for Plant Expansion	$ 60,000
Unappropriated Retained Earnings	700,000
	$760,000

A summary of the year's activities is given below.

Cash dividends declared and paid on preferred stock	$ 30,000
Cash dividends declared and paid on common stock	100,000
Net income for the year	300,000

Required:

Prepare a statement of retained earnings for the year ended December 31, 20-2.

CHAPTER 22
CORPORATIONS: BONDS

LEARNING OBJECTIVES

Chapter 22 continues the discussion of corporations and covers bonds—types of bonds, ways bonds differ from common stock, and determining sales price; bonds issued at face value; bonds issued at a premium; bonds issued at a discount; bond redemption; and bond sinking funds.

Objective 1. Describe the types of bonds, ways bonds differ from common stock, and how the sales price of bonds is determined.

Bonds are long-term obligations of the corporation. Bondholders are creditors who hold this type of corporate debt. **Mortgage bonds** are secured by property. **Unsecured bonds** are issued on the general credit of the corporation rather than on the security of specific assets. **Term bonds** all have the same maturity date; **serial bonds** are issued in a series so a portion matures each year; **convertible bonds** can be exchanged for stock; and **callable bonds** can be redeemed before maturity. **Registered bonds** have ownership recorded in corporate records (name and address of each owner), while **coupon bonds** generally do not.

Bonds differ from common stock in many ways. Bonds are owned by creditors, are liabilities with limited lives, require interest and **principal** payments, have deductible interest expenses, and provide a **leverage** opportunity.

Bonds will sell at a price based on the **stated rate** of interest on the bonds relative to the current **market rate**. If current market rates are higher than the stated rate, bonds will sell at a **discount**; if current market rates are lower than the stated rate, bonds will sell at a **premium**.

Objective 2. Account for bonds issued at face value.

Bonds issued at **face value** sell for the principal amount of the bonds. Cash is debited, and Bonds Payable is credited for the full amount. Semiannual interest is calculated by taking principal times rate times 1/2 year. A year-end adjustment is made for interest accrued but not yet paid (debiting Bond Interest Expense and crediting Bond Interest Payable). This entry normally is reversed at the beginning of the next year.

Objective 3. Account for bonds issued at a premium.

Bonds issued at a premium are sold for more than the principal amount of the bonds. Cash is debited for the cash received; Bonds Payable is credited for the principal amount; and Premium on Bonds Payable is credited for the amount above principal. Semiannual interest is calculated in the same manner as for bonds issued at face value but is reduced by a proportionate amount of the premium received when the bonds were issued. (This is **amortization** of the premium.) The year-end adjustment recognizes interest expense less the proportionate amount of premium. This entry is reversed at the beginning of the next year.

Objective 4. Account for bonds issued at a discount.

Bonds issued at a discount are sold for less than the principal amount of the bonds. Cash is debited for the cash received; Bonds Payable is credited for the principal amount; and Discount on Bonds Payable is debited for the amount below principal. Semiannual interest is calculated in the same manner as for bonds issued at face value but is increased by a proportionate amount of the discount. (This is amortization of the discount.) The year-end adjustment recognizes interest expense plus the proportionate amount of discount. This entry is reversed at the beginning of the next year.

Objective 5. Account for bond redemption and bond sinking funds.

Bonds are redeemed at face value at maturity; any premium or discount has been amortized. Therefore, Bonds Payable is debited, and Cash is credited for the face value of the bonds.

Sometimes, however, bonds are redeemed before maturity. If bonds that were sold at face value are redeemed above 100, a loss occurs. If they are redeemed below 100, a gain occurs. If bonds were originally issued at a premium, unamortized premium must be recognized at the time of redemption. If bonds were originally issued at a discount, unamortized discount must be recognized when the bonds are redeemed. To determine the gain or loss on redemption of the bonds, compare the redemption price with the **carrying value** of the bonds.

Bond sinking funds are accumulations of periodic cash deposits made to provide for redemption of bonds at maturity. This cash is invested and accumulates earnings. Any cash left in the sinking fund after bonds are redeemed is returned to the corporation.

REVIEW QUESTIONS

Instructions: Analyze each of the following items carefully before writing your answer in the column at the right.

		Question	Answer
LO 1	**1.**	A(n) ________ is a written promise to pay a specific sum of money at a specific future date.	________________
LO 1	**2.**	A(n) ________ bond is backed by specific corporate assets.	________________
LO 1	**3.**	Bonds secured by corporate property such as real estate are called ________ bonds.	________________
LO 1	**4.**	A(n) ________ bond is backed by the general credit of the corporation; these bonds are called ________ bonds.	________________
LO 1	**5.**	The amount to be paid to the bondholder at maturity is called the ________.	________________
LO 1	**6.**	________ bonds all have the same maturity date.	________________
LO 1	**7.**	________ bonds are issued so a certain amount of the bonds mature each year.	________________
LO 1	**8.**	________ bonds can be exchanged for capital stock.	________________
LO 1	**9.**	________ bonds can be redeemed before maturity.	________________
LO 1	**10.**	Bonds whose ownership is recorded in the corporate records are called ________ bonds.	________________
LO 1	**11.**	Bonds whose ownership generally is not recorded in corporate records are called ________, or bearer, bonds.	________________
LO 1	**12.**	The current, or ________, rate of interest is what is available on similar investment opportunities.	________________
LO 1	**13.**	When bonds are sold at a price less than face value, the difference is called a(n) ________.	________________
LO 1	**14.**	When bonds are sold at a price greater than face value, the difference is called a(n) ________.	________________
LO 1	**15.**	Earning a greater rate of return on funds you have borrowed than the rate you paid for those funds is known as ________. .	________________

LO 2 **16.** Year-end adjustments are made for interest on bonds by debiting Bond Interest Expense and crediting ________. .... ____________

LO 2 **17.** Year-end adjustments are ______ at the beginning of the next year. ____________

LO 3/4 **18.** Bond premiums and discounts are written off, or ________, over the life of the bonds. .... ____________

LO 5 **19.** When bonds are redeemed before maturity, ________ premium or discount on bonds must be recognized. .... ____________

LO 5 **20.** Cash funds that are accumulated to redeem bonds at maturity are called ________. .... ____________

EXERCISES

Exercise 1 (LO 2) BONDS ISSUED AT FACE VALUE

Prepare the general journal entries for the issuance of the following bonds at face value, the first interest payment on the bonds, and the first year-end adjustment for the bonds.

Date of issue and sale:	April 1, 20-1
Principal amount:	$400,000
Denomination of bonds:	$1,000
Life of bonds:	10 years
Stated interest rate:	9%, payable semiannually on September 30 and March 31

(a) Issuance of bonds

2							2
3							3
4							4
5							5

(b) Interest payment

10							10
11							11
12							12
13							13

(c) Year-end adjustment

18							18
19							19
20							20
21							21

Exercise 2 (LO 3) BONDS ISSUED AT A PREMIUM

1. Prepare the general journal entries for the issuance of the following bonds at a premium, the first interest payment and premium amortization, and the first year-end adjustment.

Date of issue and sale:	March 1, 20-1
Principal amount:	$500,000
Sale price of bonds:	103
Denomination of bonds:	$1,000
Life of bonds:	10 years
Stated interest rate:	8%, payable semiannually on August 31 and February 28

(a) Issuance of bonds

(b) Interest payment and premium amortization

(c) Year-end adjustment

2. Prepare the bonds payable section of a partial balance sheet as of December 31, 20-1.

Exercise 3 (LO 4) BONDS ISSUED AT A DISCOUNT

Prepare the general journal entries for the issuance of the following bonds at a discount, the first interest payment and discount amortization, and the first year-end adjustment.

Date of issue and sale:	April 1, 20-1
Principal amount:	$600,000
Sale price of bonds:	96
Denomination of bonds:	$1,000
Life of bonds:	20 years
Stated interest rate:	6%, payable semiannually on September 30 and March 31

(a) Issuance of bonds

(b) Interest payment and discount amortization

(c) Year-end adjustment

Exercise 4 (LO 5) BOND SINKING FUNDS AND REDEMPTION

Prepare the journal entries to record the following initial sinking fund deposit, the first year's earnings for the sinking fund, the redemption of the bonds, and the return of excess cash to the corporation.

Besel Corporation pays $38,000 into a bond sinking fund each year for the future redemption of bonds. During the first year, the fund earns $3,050. When the bonds mature, there is a balance in the sinking fund of $410,500, of which $400,000 is used to redeem the bonds, which were originally issued at face value.

(a) Initial sinking fund deposit

(b) First year's earnings

(c) Redemption of bonds

(d) Return of excess cash

PROBLEMS

Problem 5 (LO 2/5) BONDS ISSUED AT FACE VALUE WITH SINKING FUND

Required:

Based on the following information, prepare general journal entries for Williams Electric. Label the entries (a) through (j).

Date of issue and sale:	April 1
Principal amount:	$500,000
Sale price of bonds:	100
Denomination of bonds:	$1,000
Life of bonds:	10 years
Stated interest rate:	9%, payable semiannually on April 1 and October 1
Sinking fund requirement:	$35,000 per year
Sinking fund earnings, year 1:	$3,000

(a) Issuance of bonds.
(b) Deposit to sinking fund, year 1.
(c) Earnings of sinking fund, year 1.
(d) Interest payment on the bonds for year 1.
(e) Year-end adjustment on the bonds for year 1.
(f) Reversing entry for the beginning of year 2.
(g) Interest payments on the bonds for year 2.
(h) Year-end adjustment on the bonds for year 2.
(i) Redemption at maturity from the sinking fund.
(j) Return of excess cash of $1,850 from the sinking fund to the corporation.

GENERAL JOURNAL PAGE

	DATE	DESCRIPTION	POST. REF.	DEBIT	CREDIT	
1						1
2						2
3						3
4						4
5						5
6						6
7						7
8						8
9						9
10						10
11						11
12						12
13						13
14						14
15						15

Problem 5 (Concluded)

GENERAL JOURNAL

PAGE

DATE		DESCRIPTION	POST. REF.	DEBIT	CREDIT

Name ______________________________

Problem 6 (LO 3/5) BONDS ISSUED AT A PREMIUM, AND REDEMPTION

Required:

Based on the following information, prepare general journal entries for Mastin Mercantile. Label the entries (a) through (h).

Date of issue and sale:	March 1
Principal amount:	$600,000
Sale price of bonds:	104
Denomination of bonds:	$1,000
Life of bonds:	20 years
Stated interest rate:	6%, payable semiannually on March 1 and September 1

(a) Issuance of bonds.
(b) Interest payment and premium amortization on the bonds on September 1, year 1.
(c) Year-end adjustment on the bonds for year 1.
(d) Reversing entry for the beginning of year 2.
(e) Interest payments and premium amortizations on the bonds on March 1 and September 1, year 2.
(f) Year-end adjustment on the bonds for year 2.
(g) Reversing entry for beginning of year 3.
(h) Redemption of $60,000 of the bonds on March 1 of year 3 at 106.
(*Hint*: Two full years of bond premium have been amortized to this point.)

GENERAL JOURNAL PAGE

	DATE	DESCRIPTION	POST. REF.	DEBIT	CREDIT	
1						1
2						2
3						3
4						4
5						5
6						6
7						7
8						8
9						9
10						10
11						11
12						12
13						13
14						14
15						15
16						16
17						17
18						18
19						19

Problem 6 (Concluded)

GENERAL JOURNAL

PAGE

DATE		DESCRIPTION	POST. REF.	DEBIT	CREDIT

Problem 7 (LO 4/5) BONDS ISSUED AT A DISCOUNT, AND REDEMPTION

Required:

Based on the following information, prepare general journal entries for RPT Consulting. Label the entries (a) through (k).

Date of issue and sale:	April 1
Principal amount:	$400,000
Sale price of bonds:	99
Denomination of bonds:	$1,000
Life of bonds:	10 years
Stated interest rate:	8% payable semiannually on April 1 and October 1

(a) Issuance of the bonds.
(b) Interest payment and discount amortization on the bonds on October 1, year 1.
(c) Year-end adjustment on the bonds for year 1.
(d) Reversing entry for the beginning of year 2.
(e) Interest payments and discount amortizations on the bonds on April 1 and October 1, year 2.
(f) Year-end adjustment on the bonds for year 2.
(g) Reversing entry for beginning of year 3.
(h) Interest payments and discount amortizations on the bonds on April 1 and October 1, year 3.
(i) Year-end adjustment on the bonds for year 3.
(j) Reversing entry for beginning of year 4.
(k) Redemption of $80,000 of the bonds on April 1 of year 4 at 97.
(*Hint*: Three full years of bond discount have been amortized at this point.)

GENERAL JOURNAL

PAGE

	DATE		DESCRIPTION	POST. REF.	DEBIT	CREDIT	
1							1
2							2
3							3
4							4
5							5
6							6
7							7
8							8
9							9
10							10
11							11
12							12
13							13
14							14
15							15
16							16

Problem 7 (Continued)

GENERAL JOURNAL

PAGE

	DATE		DESCRIPTION	POST. REF.	DEBIT	CREDIT	
1							1
2							2
3							3
4							4
5							5
6							6
7							7
8							8
9							9
10							10
11							11
12							12
13							13
14							14
15							15
16							16
17							17
18							18
19							19
20							20
21							21
22							22
23							23
24							24
25							25
26							26
27							27
28							28
29							29
30							30
31							31
32							32
33							33

Problem 7 (Concluded)

GENERAL JOURNAL

PAGE

	DATE	DESCRIPTION	POST. REF.	DEBIT	CREDIT	
1						1
2						2
3						3
4						4
5						5
6						6
7						7
8						8
9						9
10						10
11						11
12						12
13						13
14						14
15						15
16						16
17						17
18						18
19						19
20						20
21						21
22						22
23						23
24						24
25						25
26						26
27						27
28						28
29						29
30						30
31						31
32						32
33						33

CHAPTER 22 APPENDIX EFFECTIVE INTEREST METHOD

APPENDIX LEARNING OBJECTIVES

In Chapter 22, you learned how to amortize premium and discount on bonds payable using the straight-line method. In this appendix, we demonstrate the **effective interest method**. The effective interest rate is the market rate of interest on the date the bonds are issued. This rate is used to determine the interest expense and premium or discount amortization each period.

Objective 1. Amortize premium on bonds payable using the effective interest method.

The beginning-of-period carrying value of the bonds times the **effective interest rate** is the **effective interest expense**. The cash interest payment minus the effective interest expense is the amount of premium to be amortized for the period.

Objective 2. Amortize discount on bonds payable using the effective interest method.

The beginning-of-period carrying value of the bonds times the effective interest rate is the effective interest expense. The effective interest expense minus the cash interest payment is the amount of discount to be amortized for the period.

APPENDIX EXERCISES AND PROBLEMS

Apx. Exercise 1 (LO 1) BOND PREMIUM AMORTIZATION—EFFECTIVE INTEREST METHOD

On May 1, Urban Developers issued $100,000, 9%, 10-year bonds for $106,796 when the market rate was 8%. Prepare the general journal entry for the first semiannual interest payment and bond premium amortization on November 1, using the effective interest method.

GENERAL JOURNAL PAGE

1							1
2							2
3							3
4							4

Apx. Exercise 2 (LO 2) BOND DISCOUNT AMORTIZATION—EFFECTIVE INTEREST METHOD

On May 1, Schultz Inc. issued $350,000, 9%, 10-year bonds for $328,191 when the market rate was 10%. Prepare the general journal entry for the first semiannual interest payment and bond discount amortization on November 1, using the effective interest method.

GENERAL JOURNAL PAGE

1							1
2							2
3							3
4							4

Apx. Problem 3 (LO 1) BOND PREMIUM AMORTIZATION

Summer Company sold an issue of $600,000, 10%, 10-year bonds for $639,025 on March 1. The interest is payable semiannually on September 1 and March 1. The market rate of interest at the time the bonds were issued was 9%. Journalize the following transactions (round all amounts to the nearest dollar).

Sept. 1	Paid the first semiannual interest payment and amortized the bond premium, using the effective interest method.
Dec. 31	Made the adjusting entry for bond interest accrued and amortization of the bond premium from September 1. (*Hint*: Use the effective interest rate for the four-month period from September 1–December 31.)
Jan. 2	Reversed the adjusting entry for bond interest accrued and bond premium amortization as of December 31.
Mar. 1	Paid the second semiannual interest payment and amortized the bond premium.

GENERAL JOURNAL

PAGE

	DATE	DESCRIPTION	POST. REF.	DEBIT	CREDIT	
1						1
2						2
3						3
4						4
5						5
6						6
7						7
8						8
9						9
10						10
11						11
12						12
13						13
14						14
15						15
16						16
17						17
18						18

Apx. Problem 4 (LO 2) BOND DISCOUNT AMORTIZATION

Willis Enterprises sold an issue of $90,000, 9%, 10-year bonds for $84,393 on April 1. The interest is payable semiannually on October 1 and April 1. The market rate of interest at the time the bonds were issued was 10%. Journalize the following transactions (round all amounts to the nearest dollar).

Oct. 1	Paid the first semiannual interest payment and amortized the bond discount, using the effective interest method.
Dec. 31	Made the adjusting entry for bond interest accrued and amortization of the bond discount from October 1. (*Hint*: Use the effective interest rate for the three-month period from October 1–December 31.)
Jan. 2	Reversed the adjusting entry for bond interest accrued and bond discount amortization as of December 31.
Apr. 1	Paid the second semiannual interest payment and amortized the bond discount.

GENERAL JOURNAL

PAGE

DATE	DESCRIPTION	POST. REF.	DEBIT	CREDIT

CHAPTER 23
STATEMENT OF CASH FLOWS

LEARNING OBJECTIVES

Understanding the sources and uses of cash is critical to the operation and evaluation of a business. In Chapter 23, you learned how to prepare and interpret a statement of cash flows. Here we review the most important concepts and provide additional questions, exercises, and problems for you to solve.

Objective 1. Explain the purpose of the statement of cash flows.

The managers of a business have two principal objectives. One is to generate profits (net income), and the other is to generate enough cash from operating activities to pay operating expenditures, make investments, and retire debt. Businesses can borrow money to buy plant and equipment. However, in the long run, the debt must be paid using cash generated from operating activities.

Under the accrual basis of accounting, revenues are recorded when earned, regardless of when the cash is received. Revenue is considered earned when a performance obligation has been satisfied. Expenses are recorded when incurred, regardless of when cash is paid. Therefore, the income statement may not reflect the true nature of the cash flows. The **statement of cash flows** provides information on where the cash came from and how it was used.

Objective 2. Define operating, investing, and financing activities and describe transactions for each type of activity.

The statement of cash flows is divided into three major categories:

(1) operating activities,
(2) investing activities, and
(3) financing activities.

The sum of the cash generated or used by each of the three activities should equal the difference between the beginning and ending balance of the cash account.

Operating activities include transactions from activities associated with selling a product or providing a service and are related to the revenues and expenses reported on the income statement. Typical transactions are those involving cash receipts from the sale of goods or services, payments for the acquisition of inventory, payments to employees and the government, payments for interest on loans, dividends and interest received on investments, and payments to suppliers and for other expenses.

Investing activities are those transactions involving the purchase and sale of long-term assets, buying and selling debt and equity securities, lending money, and collecting the principal on the related loans.

Financing activities are those transactions dealing with the exchange of cash between the firm and its owners (stockholders) and creditors. Typical transactions are those involving payment of dividends to stockholders, proceeds from issuing stocks and bonds, proceeds from borrowing money through the signing of a mortgage, repayment of the principal on loans, and payments to purchase treasury stock.

Objective 3. Describe the information needed to prepare a statement of cash flows.

To prepare the statement of cash flows, balance sheets for the beginning and end of the period, as well as an income statement and statement of retained earnings for the period, are needed. Further, any additional information on major cash transactions is useful.

Objective 4. Describe the direct and indirect methods of reporting cash flows from operating activities.

Under the **indirect method**, net income is reported first on the statement of cash flows as the primary source of cash from operating activities. However, this amount must be adjusted for transactions that affect net income *and* cash flows from operating activities, but by different amounts. As shown below, these differences are related to:

- changes in current assets and current liabilities related to operating activities,
- noncash expenses (depreciation), and
- events that impact net income, but are not associated with operating activities (gains and losses).

These adjustments are added to or subtracted from net income to compute net cash provided by or used by operating activities. Under the **direct method**, revenues and expenses reported on the income statement are adjusted to reflect the amount of cash received or paid for each item. These adjusted revenues and expenses are reported on the statement of cash flows. The sum of these cash flows is equal to net cash provided or used by operating activities. Of course, the results of the two methods are the same. Net cash provided or used by operating activities must be the same amount under both methods. A comparison of the two methods is provided below.

Indirect Method	Direct Method		
Net income	Sales	± Change in Accounts Receivable	= Cash collected from customers
± Adjustments for changes in current assets related to operating activities	Interest Revenue	± Change in Interest Receivable	= Cash received for interest
	Other Operating Revenue	± Change in Unearned Revenues	= Cash received for other operating revenues
± Adjustments for changes in current liabilities related to operating activities	Cost of Goods Sold	± Change in Inventory and Accounts Payable	= Cash paid to suppliers
± Adjustments for noncash expenses	Wages Expense	± Change in Wages Payable	= Cash paid to employees
± Adjustments for items that impact net income, but are not related to operating activities (gains/losses)	Operating Expenses	± Change in Accrued Liabilities and Prepaid Expenses	= Cash paid for operating expenses
	Interest Expense	± Change in Interest Payable	= Cash paid for interest
	Tax Expense	± Change in Taxes Payable	= Cash paid for taxes
= Net cash provided/used by operating activities	⟵ **Same Results** ⟶		= Net cash provided/used by operating activities

Objective 5. Describe the effects of changes in current assets and current liabilities on cash from operating activities under the indirect method.

The effects of changes in current assets and current liabilities related to operating activities on cash flows from operating activities are shown below.

Change in Current Asset or Current Liability Related to Operating Activities	Impact on Cash Flows from Operating Activities
Increase in Current Assets Decrease in Current Liabilities	↓
Decrease in Current Assets Increase in Current Liabilities	↑

Objective 6. Prepare a statement of cash flows under the indirect method using T accounts and including adjustments for current assets and current liabilities related to operations.

Basic steps to prepare a statement of cash flows:

STEP 1 Compute the change in cash.

STEP 2 Set up T accounts with the beginning and ending balances for all noncash balance sheet accounts.

STEP 3 Compute cash flows from operating activities by:
(a) Reporting net income as the primary source of cash from operating activities.
(b) Adjusting net income for changes in current assets and current liabilities related to operating activities.

STEP 4 Identify cash flows from investing activities.

STEP 5 Identify cash flows from financing activities.

STEP 6 Prepare a statement of cash flows and verify the accuracy of the statement.

T accounts are very helpful when preparing the statement of cash flows under the indirect method because they allow us to use debits and credits to guide the preparation of the statement. Let's consider a firm with the T accounts provided below.

Accounts Receivable

	Debit	Credit	
BB	5		
(1)	5		
EB	10		

Inventory

	Debit	Credit	
BB	30		
		10	(2)
EB	20		

Accounts Payable

	Debit	Credit	
		20	BB
(3)	12		
		8	EB

Wages Payable

	Debit	Credit	
		15	BB
		3	(4)
		18	EB

Cash flows from operating activities:		
Net income		$ 100
Increase in accounts receivable	(1)	(5)
Decrease in inventory	(2)	10
Decrease in accounts payable	(3)	(12)
Increase in wages payable	(4)	3
Net cash provided by operating activities		$ 96

Cash

Operating Activities	Debit	Credit	
Net income	100		
		5	(1)
(2)	10		
		12	(3)
(4)	3		
Cash from operating activities	96		

BB: Beginning Balance

EB: Ending Balance

As discussed earlier, the increase in Accounts Receivable and the decrease in Accounts Payable reduce cash from operating activities. This concept is reinforced through the use of debits and credits. The debits to Accounts Receivable ($5) and Accounts Payable ($12) are offset by credits to the cash account. Of course, these credits reduce cash.

On the other hand, the decrease in Inventory and the increase in Wages Payable increase cash from operating activities. Again, this concept is reinforced through the use of debits and credits. The credits to Inventory ($10) and Wages Payable ($3) are offset by debits to the cash account. As you know, debits increase cash.

Now, we can use the Cash T account to prepare the statement of cash flows. Net income is entered first in the Cash T account and listed first under cash flows from operating activities because it is the primary source of cash from operating activities. Net income, however, must be adjusted for the changes in current assets and current liabilities. Using the Cash T account, these adjustments are simple. The debits to the Cash T account [entries (2) and (4)] increase cash and are added to net income on the statement of cash flows. The credits to the Cash T account [entries (1) and (3)] reduce cash and are subtracted from net income to compute cash from operating activities. To check the accuracy of this process, cash from operating activities ($96) on the statement is equal to the balance of the Cash T account ($96).

Objective 7. Prepare a statement of cash flows under the indirect method including adjustments when the company:
a. defines cash as "cash and cash equivalents,"
b. reports depreciation expense,
c. reports gains or losses on transactions not related to operating activities,
d. has noncash investing and financing activities, and
e. provides supplemental disclosures of cash flows.

A **cash equivalent** is a short-term investment that is readily convertible to a *known* amount of cash. Thus, when cash is needed, the investment can be readily and easily liquidated. Examples of cash equivalents are short-term investments in government notes and money market funds. Though the statement is titled the statement of cash flows, we actually include cash equivalents in the definition of cash to explain why cash and cash equivalents increased or decreased.

Depreciation expense reduces net income, but has no effect on cash. This is known as a **noncash expense**. Thus, as shown below, it must be added back to net income to compute cash from operating activities.

Dennis Enterprises
Statement of Cash Flows
For Year Ended December 31, 20-2

Cash flows from operating activities:		
Net income	$ 100	
Depreciation expense	5	
Loss on sale of equipment	10	
Gain on sale of building	(20)	
Net cash provided by operating activities		$ 95
Cash flows from investing activities:		
Sold equipment	$ 50	
Sold building	100	
Total cash provided by investing activities		150
Cash flows from financing activities:		
Retired bond payable	$ (100)	
Issued common stock	50	
Net cash used for financing activities		(50)
Net increase (decrease) in cash and cash equivalents		$195
Cash and cash equivalents, January 1, 20-2		80
Cash and cash equivalents, December 31, 20-2		$275
Schedule of Noncash Investing and Financing Activities:		
Acquired building by signing a mortgage payable		$200
Supplemental Disclosures of Cash Flow Information:		
Cash paid during the year for:		
Interest		$ 10
Income taxes		40

Gains and losses on the sale of property, plant, and equipment are included on the income statement and in the calculation of net income. However, these gains and losses are related to investing, not operating, activities. Net income is used as the primary source of cash from operating activities. Thus, it must be adjusted for these gains and losses. Since gains increase net income, they must be subtracted when computing cash from operating activities. Since losses reduce net income, they must be added. One such adjustment is illustrated on the previous page.

Some investing and financing activities involve no cash flows but represent a significant change in the firm's financial position. These events are called **noncash investing and financing activities.** A schedule of these transactions is presented at the bottom of the statement of cash flows. Examples of this type of transaction include acquiring property, plant, and equipment by issuing debt and retiring debt by issuing common stock. As shown on page 378, Dennis Enterprises acquired a building by signing a mortgage payable.

Firms using the indirect method are required to disclose the amount of cash paid for interest and income taxes. This information is also reported in a separate section of the statement, "supplemental disclosures of cash flow information." As shown on page 378, Dennis paid $10 for interest and $40 for income taxes.

Objective 8. Interpret the statement of cash flows.

The purpose of the statement of cash flows is to provide information on the sources and uses of cash. The most important indicator of financial health is the net cash flow from operating activities. Operating activities should be generating a good, healthy cash flow, indicating that the business can cover its operating expenses and pay all of its bills on time. A chronic inability to generate positive cash flows from operations is a sure sign of financial instability.

REVIEW QUESTIONS

Instructions: Analyze each of the following items carefully before writing your answer in the column at the right.

	Question	Answer
LO 1	1. The managers of a business have the dual objectives of generating ________ and ________.	________ ________
LO 1	2. The income statement reports on the profitability of the firm by matching revenues and expenses on a(n) ________ basis.	________
LO 1	3. The purpose of the statement of cash flows is to provide information on the ________ and ________ of cash.	________ ________
LO 2	4. The statement of cash flows categorizes all cash flows into what three major types of activities?	________ ________ ________
LO 2	5. Transactions involving the purchase and sale of long-term assets are called ________ activities.	________

LO 2 **6.** Transactions involving the payments of dividends to stockholders and the proceeds from the issuance of stock and bonds are called ________ activities. .... ____________________

LO 2 **7.** Transactions involving the payment for acquisition of inventory, payment of salary to employees, and cash receipts from sale of goods or services are called ________ activities. .... ____________________

LO 2 **8.** The receipt of a cash dividend from an investment is classified as a(n) ________ activity. .... ____________________

LO 2 **9.** The receipt of interest from an investment and the payment of interest on a loan are classified as ________ activities. .... ____________________

LO 2/7 **10.** The sum of the cash generated or used by each of the three activities should equal the difference between the beginning and ending balance(s) of the ________ account(s). .... ____________________

LO 3 **11.** The information needed to prepare a statement of cash flows includes what four items? .... ____________________

____

____

____

LO 4 **12.** The two methods that are used to compute cash generated from operating activities are the ________ method and the ________ method. .... ____________________

____

LO 5/6 **13.** A decrease in accrued interest receivable is (added to/deducted from) net income to determine cash generated from operating activities. .... ____________________

LO 5/6 **14.** An increase in accrued interest payable is (added to/deducted from) net income to determine cash generated from operating activities. .... ____________________

LO 5/6 **15.** If accounts receivable increased during the year, this amount is (added to/deducted from) net income to determine cash generated from operating activities. .... ____________________

LO 5/6 **16.** An increase in inventory during the year should be (added to/deducted from) net income to determine cash generated from operating activities. .... ____________________

LO 5/6 **17.** A decrease in accounts payable during the year should be (added to/deducted from) net income to determine cash generated from operating activities. .... ____________________

LO 7 **18.** Depreciation expense is (added to/deducted from) net income to determine cash generated from operating activities. .... ____________________

LO 6 **19.** When using debits and credits to help prepare the statement of cash flows, debits represent what two things? .... ______________ ______________

LO 6 **20.** When using debits and credits to help prepare the statement of cash flows, credits represent what two things? .... ______________ ______________

LO 7 **21.** Supplemental disclosures of cash flows under the indirect method include what two things? .... ______________ ______________

LO 7 **22.** The issuance of common stock to retire a bond is classified as a ________. .... ______________

LO 7 **23.** A gain on the sale of a building should be ________ when preparing the statement of cash flows. .... ______________

LO 7 **24.** To earn a return on otherwise idle cash, many firms invest in short-term, highly liquid investments known as ________. .... ______________

LO 8 **25.** Probably the most important indicator of financial health is the net cash flow from ________ activities. .... ______________

EXERCISES

Exercise 1 (LO 2) IDENTIFICATION OF OPERATING, INVESTING, AND FINANCING ACTIVITIES

Indicate under which heading (operating activity, investing activity, or financing activity) the following cash flows would be categorized on the statement of cash flows:

1. Issued $50,000 of common stock. ______________
2. Paid monthly salaries of $35,624. ______________
3. Purchased 50 shares of treasury stock. ______________
4. Collected the $70,000 principal of a loan made to another company. ______________
5. Collected interest of $5,600 on the above loan. ______________
6. Purchased a new piece of equipment for $46,500. ______________
7. Purchased 500 shares of another company's common stock for $2,500. ______________
8. Received $600 in dividends from the common stock. ______________
9. Paid dividends of $40,000 to stockholders. ______________
10. Paid quarterly FICA tax. ______________

Exercise 2 (LO 6) CHANGE IN CASH

The information provided below was taken from the December 31 comparative balance sheet of Proc Company. Based on this information, compute the change in cash that would be explained on a statement of cash flows for 20-2.

	20-2	20-1
Current assets:		
Cash	$ 87,500	$ 78,600
Accounts receivable	154,700	164,500
Merchandise inventory	226,800	243,600
Total current assets	$469,000	$486,700

Exercise 3 (LO 5/6) ADJUSTING NET INCOME FOR CHANGES IN CURRENT ASSETS

The information provided below was taken from the December 31 financial statements of Todd Company. Based on this information, compute cash generated from operating activities during 20-2.

	20-2	20-1
Accounts receivable	$154,700	$164,500
Merchandise inventory	250,800	243,600

Net income for 20-2 was $300,000.

Exercise 4 (LO 5/6) ADJUSTING NET INCOME FOR CHANGES IN CURRENT ASSETS AND CURRENT LIABILITIES

The information provided below was taken from the December 31 financial statements of Simmons Company. Based on this information, compute the cash from operating activities for 20-2.

	20-2	20-1
Accounts receivable	$154,700	$164,500
Merchandise inventory	226,800	243,600
Prepaid rent	26,000	24,000
Accounts payable (suppliers of merchandise)	156,000	145,000
Income tax payable	10,000	15,000

Net income for 20-2 was $200,000.

Exercise 5 (LO 7) ADJUSTING NET INCOME FOR NONCASH EXPENSES

After adjusting net income for changes in current assets and current liabilities, Vozniak Pharmacy's cash from operating activities is $225,000. However, Vozniak reports $20,000 in depreciation expense and $35,000 for patent amortization for the year. Compute cash from operating activities after considering the impact of noncash expenses.

Exercise 6 (LO 6) CASH FLOWS FROM INVESTING AND FINANCING ACTIVITIES

The information provided below was taken from the December 31 financial statements of Henninger Company. Based on this information, compute the cash flow from investing and financing activities during 20-2.

	20-2	20-1
Property, plant, and equipment:		
Land	$ 30,000	$ 20,000
Long-term liabilities:		
Notes payable	200,000	150,000
Mortgage payable	325,000	330,000

Exercise 7 (LO 7) CHANGE IN CASH AND CASH EQUIVALENTS

The information provided below was taken from the December 31 comparative balance sheet of Roedl Company. Based on this information, compute the change in cash and cash equivalents that would be explained on a statement of cash flows for 20-2.

	20-2	20-1
Current assets:		
Cash	$ 87,500	$ 78,600
Government notes	10,000	12,000
Accounts receivable	135,700	144,900
Merchandise inventory	255,800	276,600
Total current assets	$489,000	$512,100

Exercise 8 (LO 7) GAINS AND LOSSES ON THE SALE OF LONG-TERM ASSETS

The income statement for Kenlawn Nursery is shown below. Assume that all revenues and expenses were for cash and that land was sold for $15,000. There were no other investing or financing activities during the year. The Cash balances at the beginning and end of the year were $10,000 and $45,000, respectively. Prepare a statement of cash flows.

Kenlawn Nursery
Income Statement
For Year Ended December 31, 20-2

Sales (all cash)	$80,000
Wages expense (all cash)	60,000
Operating income	$20,000
Loss on sale of land	(2,000)
Net income	$18,000

Exercise 9 (LO 7) CALCULATION OF CASH GENERATED FROM OPERATING ACTIVITIES

Information from the December 31 financial statements of Pinehurst Corporation is listed below.

	20-2	20-1
Cash	$ 76,320	$ 72,480
Accounts receivable	184,500	175,200
Merchandise inventory	225,300	215,700
Supplies	12,500	14,800
Prepaid insurance	18,200	16,300
Accounts payable (suppliers of merchandise)	132,000	140,000
Accrued wages payable	2,200	3,100
Accrued payroll taxes	3,200	2,700

Net sales	$625,000
Cost of goods sold	330,000
Wages expense	125,500
Depreciation expense	45,000
Supplies expense	45,500
Payroll taxes expense	10,200
Insurance expense	22,500
Net income	$ 46,300

Based on the information provided, prepare a partial statement of cash flows reporting cash flows from operating activities.

Exercise 10 (LO 7) NONCASH INVESTING AND FINANCING ACTIVITIES

The Wantz Factory issued a $20,000, five-year note payable to acquire new furniture. Show how this transaction is reported on a statement of cash flows.

Exercise 11 (LO 7) CASH PAID FOR INTEREST AND INCOME TAXES

Based on the following information taken from the December 31 financial statements of Midex Company, compute the cash paid for interest and income taxes:

	20-2	20-1
Accrued interest payable	$ 2,400	$ 3,200
Income tax payable	15,500	11,300
Interest expense, 20-2	8,200	
Income tax expense, 20-2	30,300	

PROBLEMS

Problem 12 (LO 6) CASH GENERATED FROM OPERATING ACTIVITIES

The following information was taken from the financial statements of Roget's Bottling Company:

Roget's Bottling Company
Income Statement
For Year Ended December 31, 20-2

Net sales	$800,000
Cost of goods sold	450,000
Gross profit	$350,000
Operating expenses	119,000
Income before taxes	$231,000
Income tax expense	81,000
Net income	$150,000

Roget's Bottling Company
Comparative Balance Sheet (Partial)
December 31, 20-2 and 20-1

	20-2	20-1	Increase (Decrease)
Assets			
Current assets:			
Cash	$ 60,000	$ 70,000	$(10,000)
Accounts receivable	20,000	25,000	(5,000)
Merchandise inventory	160,000	180,000	(20,000)
Total current assets	$240,000	$275,000	$(35,000)
Liabilities			
Current liabilities:			
Accounts payable	$ 40,000	$ 30,000	$ 10,000

Required: Prepare a partial statement of cash flows reporting cash flows from operating activities.

Problem 13 (LO 7) PREPARE A STATEMENT OF CASH FLOWS

The financial statements and additional information for Moles Company are shown below and on the next page.

Moles Company
Income Statement
For Year Ended December 31, 20-2

Net sales	$1,000,000
Cost of goods sold	700,000
Gross profit	$ 300,000
Operating expenses	177,000
Income before taxes	$ 123,000
Income tax expense	43,000
Net income	$ 80,000

Moles Company
Comparative Balance Sheet
December 31, 20-2 and 20-1

	20-2	20-1	Increase (Decrease)
Assets			
Current assets:			
Cash	$ 80,000	$200,000	$(120,000)
Accounts receivable	160,000	180,000	(20,000)
Merchandise inventory	180,000	200,000	(20,000)
Total current assets	$420,000	$580,000	(160,000)
Property, plant, and equipment:			
Land	$ 40,000	$ 50,000	(10,000)
Building	140,000		140,000
Equipment	100,000		100,000
Total property, plant, and equipment	$280,000	$ 50,000	230,000
Total assets	$700,000	$630,000	70,000
Liabilities			
Current liabilities:			
Accounts payable	$120,000	$180,000	(60,000)
Notes payable	60,000	50,000	10,000
Total liabilities	$180,000	$230,000	(50,000)
Stockholders' Equity			
Common stock ($5 par, 100,000 shares authorized, 50,000 and 58,000 issued)	$290,000	$250,000	40,000
Paid-in capital in excess of par—common stock	120,000	100,000	20,000
Retained earnings	110,000	50,000	60,000
Total stockholders' equity	$520,000	$400,000	120,000
Total liabilities and stockholders' equity	$700,000	$630,000	70,000

Problem 13 (Continued)

Moles Company
Statement of Retained Earnings
For Year Ended December 31, 20-2

Retained earnings, January 1, 20-2		$ 50,000
Net income	$80,000	
Less dividends	20,000	
Net increase in retained earnings		60,000
Retained earnings, December 31, 20-2		$110,000

Additional information:

1. A building costing $140,000 and equipment costing $90,000 were acquired just before the year-end. Moles Company had accumulated enough cash to cover these acquisitions.
2. Issued 8,000 shares of common stock for $7.50 per share.
3. Declared and paid cash dividends of $20,000.
4. Moles Company uses accounts payable only for amounts owed to suppliers of merchandise inventory.
5. Additional equipment was acquired by issuing a note payable for $10,000.

Required:

1. Prepare a statement of cash flows for the year ended December 31, 20-2.
2. Reconcile the cash account at the bottom of the statement of cash flows.

Problem 13 (Concluded)

1. and 2.

Problem 14 (LO 7) PREPARE A STATEMENT OF CASH FLOWS

The financial statements and additional information for the preparation of a statement of cash flows for Eubanks Corporation are provided below and on the following pages.

Eubanks Corporation
Income Statement
For Year Ended December 31, 20-2

Net sales		$1,150,250
Cost of goods sold		675,250
Gross profit		$ 475,000
Operating expenses		301,876
Operating income		$ 173,124
Other revenue and expenses:		
Interest revenue	$ 500	
Interest expense	(2,500)	
Gain on the sale of store equipment	10,000	
Loss on the retirement of bond	(3,000)	5,000
Income before taxes		$ 178,124
Income tax expense		60,000
Net income		$ 118,124

Eubanks Corporation
Statement of Retained Earnings
For Year Ended December 31, 20-2

Retained earnings, January 1, 20-2		$ 59,156
Net income	$118,124	
Less dividends	32,000	
Net increase in retained earnings		86,124
Retained earnings, December 31, 20-2		$145,280

Additional information:

1. Store equipment was sold during the year for $40,000.

Cost	$50,000
Accumulated depreciation	(20,000)
Book value	$30,000
Market value	40,000
Gain on sale of store equipment	$10,000

2. Depreciation expense was $26,000 as follows:

Store equipment	$10,000
Delivery equipment	11,250
Office equipment	4,750
	$26,000

3. A $50,000 bond payable was retired early at a loss of $3,000.

Carrying value	$50,000
Amount paid to retire bond	53,000
Loss on retirement of bond	$ (3,000)

Problem 14 (Continued)

4. The following purchases were made:

Store equipment	$23,000
Delivery equipment	32,500
Office equipment	10,025
	$65,525

5. Paid dividends of $32,000.
6. Issued 7,000 shares of common stock for $57,500.
7. Acquired office equipment by issuing a note payable for $10,000.

Required:

1. Prepare a statement of cash flows.
2. Verify the accuracy of the statement of cash flows.

Note: This problem includes a loss on the retirement of bonds which is not illustrated in the text. However, if you apply the concepts learned in the text to the retirement of bonds, you should be able to complete this problem successfully. Have fun.

Problem 14 (Continued)

Eubanks Corporation
Comparative Balance Sheet
December 31, 20-2 and 20-1

Assets	20-2		20-1		Increase (Decrease)
Current assets:					
Cash	$ 89,947		$ 53,000		$ 36,947
Government notes	1,500		5,000		(3,500)
Accrued interest receivable	75		175		(100)
Accounts receivable (net)	140,223		126,500		13,723
Merchandise inventory	161,420		168,780		(7,360)
Supplies and prepayments	10,038		6,840		3,198
Total current assets		$403,203		$360,295	42,908
Property, plant, and equipment:					
Store equipment	$ 70,000		$ 97,000		(27,000)
Less accum. depr.—store equipment	25,000	45,000	35,000	62,000	(10,000)
Delivery equipment	$112,500		$ 80,000		32,500
Less accum. depr.—delivery equipment	31,250	81,250	20,000	60,000	11,250
Office equipment	$105,000		$ 84,975		20,025
Less accum. depr.—office equipment	20,000	85,000	15,250	69,725	4,750
Total property, plant, and equipment		$211,250		$191,725	19,525
Total assets		$614,453		$552,020	62,433
Liabilities					
Current liabilities:					
Notes payable	$ 35,200		$ 29,500		5,700
Accounts payable	65,288		96,864		(31,576)
Income tax payable	16,000		20,000		(4,000)
Accrued and withheld payroll taxes	2,475		3,800		(1,325)
Accrued interest payable	210		200		10
Total current liabilities		$119,173		$150,364	(31,191)
Long-term liabilities:					
Bonds payable		—		50,000	(50,000)
Stockholders' Equity					
Common stock ($5 par, 100,000 shares authorized, 50,000 and 43,000 shares issued)	$250,000		$215,000		35,000
Paid-in capital in excess of par value—common stock	100,000		77,500		22,500
Retained earnings	145,280		59,156		86,124
Total stockholders' equity		495,280		351,656	143,624
Total liabilities and stockholders' equity		$614,453		$552,020	62,433

Problem 14 (Continued)

1. and 2. T Accounts for Indirect Method Statement of Cash Flows
Eubanks Corporation

Accrued Interest Receivable

BB	175		
EB	75		

Accounts Receivable

BB	126,500		
EB	140,223		

Merchandise Inventory

BB	168,780		
EB	161,420		

Supplies and Prepayments

BB	6,840		
EB	10,038		

Store Equipment

BB	97,000		
EB	70,000		

Accumulated Depreciation—Store Equipment

		35,000	BB
		25,000	EB

Delivery Equipment

BB	80,000		
EB	112,500		

Accumulated Depreciation—Delivery Equipment

		20,000	BB
		31,250	EB

Office Equipment

BB	84,975		
EB	105,000		

Accumulated Depreciation—Office Equipment

		15,250	BB
		20,000	EB

Notes Payable

		29,500	BB
		35,200	EB

Accounts Payable

		96,864	BB
		65,288	EB

Income Tax Payable

		20,000	BB
		16,000	EB

Accrued and Withheld Payroll Taxes

		3,800	BB
		2,475	EB

Accrued Interest Payable

		200	BB
		210	EB

Bonds Payable

		50,000	BB
		—	EB

Common Stock

		215,000	BB
		250,000	EB

Paid-In Capital in Excess of Par—Common Stock

		77,500	BB
		100,000	EB

Retained Earnings

		59,156	BB
		145,280	EB

BB: Beginning Balance
EB: Ending Balance

Hint: Be sure to reconcile all of these accounts to identify all transactions for the year.

Problem 14 (Continued)

Problem 14 (Concluded)

CHAPTER 23 APPENDIX
STATEMENT OF CASH FLOWS: THE DIRECT METHOD

APPENDIX LEARNING OBJECTIVES

The appendix to Chapter 23 illustrates the direct method of reporting cash flows from operating activities.

Objective 1. Describe the direct method of reporting cash flows from operating activities.

Under the **direct method**, revenues and expenses reported on the income statement are adjusted to reflect the amount of cash received or paid for each item. These adjusted revenues and expenses are reported on the statement of cash flows. The sum of these cash flows is equal to net cash provided or used by operating activities.

Objective 2. Prepare a schedule for the calculation of cash generated from operating activities under the direct method by adjusting revenues and expenses for changes in current assets and current liabilities associated with operations.

Under the **direct method**, revenues and expenses reported on the income statement are adjusted to reflect the amount of cash received or paid for each item. To compute the cash generated from operating activities, it is convenient to develop a schedule converting the revenues and expenses reported on the income statement to cash received or paid. Let's consider a firm with the following information:

Income Statement			Balance Sheet	BB	EB
Sales		$180	Accounts receivable	$ 5	$10
Cost of goods sold	$50		Inventory	30	20
Wages expense	30	80	Accounts payable	20	8
Net income		$100	Wages payable	15	18

BB: Beginning Balance
EB: Ending Balance

To compute cash from operating activities under the direct method, a schedule as shown below may be used. Column 1 reports the revenue or expense as reported on the income statement. Columns 2 and 3 are used for adjustments to convert the accrual basis amounts reported on the income statement to cash basis amounts on the statement of cash flows. Column 4 is used to report the cash received or paid for each line on the income statement.

Schedule for the Calculation of Cash Generated from Operating Activities

Income Statement		Additions		Deductions		Cash Flows	
Sales	$180			(1)	$ (5)	$175	Cash from customers
Cost of goods sold	50	(3)	$12	(2)	(10)	52	Cash paid to suppliers
Wages expense	30			(4)	(3)	27	Cash paid to employees
Net income	$100					$ 96	Cash from operating activities

1. Deduct the $5 increase in accounts receivable.
2. Deduct the $10 decrease in inventory.
3. Add the $12 decrease in accounts payable.
4. Deduct the $3 increase in wages payable.

You can also compute the cash paid or received by using T accounts and entries for the above revenues and expenses as shown below.

CASH FROM CUSTOMERS (1)

Cash		Accounts Receivable		Sales	
		BB 5			
(3) 175		(2) 5			180 (1)
		EB 10			

Cash from customers (175)

(3) Cash	175	
(2) Accounts Receivable	5	
(1) Sales		180

CASH PAID TO SUPPLIERS (2 & 3)

Cash		Accounts Payable		Inventory		Cost of Goods Sold	
			20 BB	BB 30			
	52 (3) ←	(3) 52	40 (2) ←	(2) 40	50 (1) ←	(1) 50	
			8 EB	EB 20			

Plug = Purchases of inventory (40)

Plug = Cash paid to suppliers (52)

(1) Cost of Goods Sold	50	
Inventory		50
(2) Inventory	40	
Accounts Payable		40
(3) Accounts Payable	52	
Cash		52

CASH PAID TO EMPLOYEES (4)

Cash		Wages Payable		Wages Expense	
			15 BB		
	27 (3)		3 (2)	(1) 30	
			18 EB		

Cash paid to employees (27)

(1) Wages Expense	30	
(2) Wages Payable		3
(3) Cash		27

BB: Beginning Balance
EB: Ending Balance

Objective 3. **Prepare a schedule for the calculation of cash generated from operating activities under the direct method, including adjustments when the company reports:**

a. **changes in current assets and current liabilities associated with operations,**
b. **depreciation expense,**
c. **gains or losses on the sale of long-term assets,**
d. **receivables and payables associated with interest revenue, interest expense, and tax expense.**

Techniques used to adjust revenues and expenses for changes in current assets and current liabilities have already been illustrated. Here, let's focus on adjustments required for noncash expenses (depreciation) and gains and losses on the sale of long-term assets. These adjustments are relatively easy if you keep in mind that we are computing **cash** generated from **operating** activities. Let's expand the above illustration to include depreciation expense and a gain on the sale of equipment. These items are in bold below.

Schedule for the Calculation of Cash Generated from Operating Activities

Income Statement		Additions		Deductions		Cash Flows	
Sales	$180			(1)	(5)	$175	Cash from customers
Cost of goods sold	50	(3)	$12	(2)	(10)	52	Cash paid to suppliers
Wages expense	30			(4)	(3)	27	Cash paid to employees
Depreciation expense	**10**			**(5)**	**(10)**		**No cash is paid for depreciation**
Gain on sale of equipment	**4**			**(6)**	**(4)**	___	**Not related to operating activities**
Net income	$ 94					$ 96	Cash from operating activities

1. Deduct the $5 increase in accounts receivable.
2. Deduct the $10 decrease in inventory.
3. Add the $12 decrease in accounts payable.
4. Deduct the $3 increase in wages payable.
5. **Deduct $10 from depreciation expense. No cash is paid for depreciation.**
6. **Deduct $4 from the gain on the sale of equipment. The gain is not related to operating activities.**

Depreciation expense and the gain are included in the calculation of net income. However, they have no effect on cash generated from operating activities. No cash is paid for depreciation expense. The gain on the sale of equipment is not related to operating activities. Thus, both amounts are adjusted to zero.

Objective 4. Prepare a statement of cash flows under the direct method.

The Cash Flows columns in the schedule for the calculation of cash from operating activities are used to prepare the statement of cash flows. As discussed earlier, the investing and financing sections of the statement of cash flows are identical under the direct and indirect methods. Thus, we will focus on the operating section here.

Let's assume that Paul Company has completed a schedule for the calculation of cash from operating activities and it includes the following:

Cash received from customers	$175
Cash paid to suppliers	52
Cash paid to employees	27
Cash paid for interest	5
Cash paid for income taxes	30
Interest received	3
Dividends received	2

This information is used to prepare the operating section of the statement of cash flows as shown on the following page.

Paul Company
Partial Statement of Cash Flows (Direct Method)
For Year Ended December 31, 20-2

Cash flows from operating activities:		
Cash received from customers	$175	
Interest received	3	
Dividends received	2	
Cash provided by operating activities		$ 180
Cash paid to suppliers of merchandise	$ (52)	
Cash paid to employees	(27)	
Cash paid for interest	(5)	
Cash paid for income taxes	(30)	
Total cash disbursed for operating activities		(114)
Net cash provided by operating activities		$ 66

REVIEW QUESTIONS

Instructions: Analyze each of the following items carefully before writing your answer in the column at the right.

	Question	Answer
LO 2	**1.** If accounts receivable increased during the year, this amount is (added to/deducted from) sales to determine the amount of cash received from customers during the year.	______________
LO 2	**2.** An increase in inventory during the year should be (added to/ deducted from) cost of goods sold to determine the cost of merchandise purchased.	______________
LO 2	**3.** A decrease in accounts payable during the year should be (added to/deducted from) cost of goods sold to determine the amount of cash paid for merchandise.	______________
LO 3	**4.** Depreciation expense is (added to/deducted from) operating expenses to compute cash paid for operating expenses.	______________
LO 3	**5.** A decrease in accrued interest receivable is (added to/deducted from) interest revenue to determine the cash received from interest revenue.	______________
LO 3	**6.** An increase in accrued interest payable is (added to/deducted from) interest expense to compute the cash paid for interest expense.	______________

EXERCISES

Apx. Exercise 1 (LO 2) CASH RECEIVED FROM CUSTOMERS

The information provided below was taken from the December 31 financial statements of Proc Company. Based on this information, compute the cash received from customers during 20-2.

	20-2	20-1
Cash	$ 87,500	$ 78,600
Accounts receivable	154,700	164,500
Merchandise inventory	226,800	243,600
Total current assets	$469,000	$486,700
Net sales, 20-2	$550,000	

Apx. Exercise 2 (LO 2) CASH PAID FOR MERCHANDISE

The information provided below was taken from the December 31 financial statements of Proc Company. Based on this information, compute the cash paid to suppliers of merchandise during 20-2.

	20-2	20-1
Cash	$ 87,500	$ 78,600
Accounts receivable	154,700	164,500
Merchandise inventory	226,800	243,600
Accounts payable (suppliers of merchandise)	156,000	145,000
Cost of goods sold, 20-2	330,000	

Apx. Exercise 3 (LO 3) SCHEDULE FOR CALCULATION OF CASH GENERATED FROM OPERATING ACTIVITIES

Information from the December 31 financial statements of Pinehurst Corporation is listed below.

	20-2	20-1
Cash	$ 76,320	$ 72,480
Accounts receivable	184,500	175,200
Merchandise inventory	225,300	215,700
Supplies	12,500	14,800
Prepaid insurance	18,200	16,300
Accounts payable (suppliers of merchandise)	132,000	140,000
Accrued wages payable	2,200	3,100
Accrued payroll taxes	3,200	2,700
Net sales, 20-2	$625,000	
Cost of goods sold, 20-2	330,000	
Wages expense	125,500	
Depreciation expense	45,000	
Supplies expense	45,500	
Payroll tax expense	10,200	
Insurance expense	22,500	

Based on the information provided, compute the following:

(a) Cash received from customers.
(b) Cash paid to suppliers of merchandise.
(c) Cash paid to employees.
(d) Cash paid for depreciation.
(e) Cash paid for insurance.
(f) Cash paid for supplies.
(g) Cash paid for payroll taxes.

Apx. Exercise 3 (Concluded)

Apx. Exercise 4 (LO 3) CASH RECEVED AND PAID FOR INTEREST

Based on the following information taken from the December 31 financial statements of Midex Company, compute the cash paid for interest expense and received from interest revenue:

	20-2	20-1
Accrued interest receivable	$ 2,400	$3,200
Accrued interest payable	1,500	1,300
Interest expense, 20-2	18,200	
Interest revenue, 20-2	10,300	

PROBLEMS

Apx. Problem 5 (LO 2) CASH GENERATED FROM OPERATING ACTIVITIES

Required:

Using the information provided in Problem 12 on page 390, prepare the following:

1. A schedule for the calculation of cash generated from operating activities for Roget's Bottling Company for the year ended December 31, 20-2.
2. A partial statement of cash flows for Roget's Bottling Company reporting cash from operating activities under the direct method for the year ended December 31, 20-2.

1.

Income Statement	Additions	Deductions	Cash Flows

Apx. Problem 5 (Concluded)

2.

Apx. Problem 6 (LO 2) CASH GENERATED FROM OPERATING ACTIVITIES

Required:

Using the information provided in Problem 13 on pages 391 and 392, prepare the following:

1. A schedule for the calculation of cash generated from operating activities for Moles Company for the year ended December 31, 20-2.
2. A statement of cash flows for Moles Company reporting cash from operating activities under the direct method for the year ended December 31, 20-2.

1.

Income Statement	Additions	Deductions	Cash Flows

Apx. Problem 6 (Concluded)

2.

Apx. Problem 7 (LO 3/4) STATEMENT OF CASH FLOWS UNDER THE DIRECT METHOD

Required:

Using the information provided in Problem 14 on pages 394-398, prepare the following:

1. A schedule for the calculation of cash generated from operating activities for Eubanks Corporation for the year ended December 31, 20-2.
2. A statement of cash flows for Eubanks Corporation prepared under the direct method for the year ended December 31, 20-2.

1. ____

____

____

Income Statement	Additions	Deductions	Cash Flows

Apx. Problem 7 (Concluded)

2.

CHAPTER 24
ANALYSIS OF FINANCIAL STATEMENTS

LEARNING OBJECTIVES

Chapter 24 explores the analysis of financial statements—horizontal and vertical analyses of the income statement and balance sheet and measures of liquidity, activity, profitability, leverage, and those related to the market. Calculating ratios is an important procedure when evaluating how the business is doing—in comparison with previous periods, other companies, industry averages, and goals.

Objective 1. Perform horizontal and vertical analyses of the income statement and balance sheet.

Horizontal analysis tracks the dollar and percentage change in each line item of the balance sheet and/or income statement across accounting periods. The earlier year is used as the base in determining the percentage change.

Vertical analysis tracks the percentage of each line item of the income statement and/or balance sheet in relation to some designated total. On the income statement, each item is shown as a percentage of net sales. On the balance sheet, assets are shown as a percentage of total assets, whereas liabilities and stockholders' equity are shown as a percentage of total liabilities and stockholders' equity.

Objective 2. Compute and explain liquidity measures.

Liquidity measures indicate the ability to meet current debts as they come due. **Working capital** is the excess of current assets over current liabilities. The **current ratio** (or **working capital ratio**) is calculated by dividing total current assets by total current liabilities. It indicates the current position of the company in terms of a ratio. The **quick** or **acid-test ratio** is another measure of liquidity; it is calculated by dividing quick assets (cash, temporary investments, and receivables) by current liabilities.

Objective 3. Compute and explain activity measures.

Activity measures offer an indication of the efficiency with which assets are being used to generate profits. **Accounts receivable turnover** measures the success of collecting accounts. It is calculated by dividing net sales on account by the average net accounts receivable. **Merchandise inventory turnover** offers an indication of the time required to sell inventory. It is calculated by dividing cost of goods sold by the average merchandise inventory. Ideally, a business would have maximum sales and minimum inventory or a large turnover rate. The larger the turnover rate, the more times inventory is purchased and sold during the year. The **asset turnover ratio** is determined by dividing net sales by average assets. It measures how efficiently assets are used to generate sales.

Objective 4. Compute and explain profitability measures.

Profitability measures indicate the ability to earn income by operating efficiently. The **profit margin ratio** (**net income ratio**) is calculated by dividing net income by net sales. It provides a measure of the net income generated by each dollar of sales. **Return on assets (ROA)** is net income divided by average assets. It compares earnings to resources. **Return on common stockholders' equity (ROE)** is net income available to common stockholders divided by average common stockholders' equity. It measures the rate of return for stockholders based on their investment. **Earnings per share of common stock** is net income available to common stockholders divided by average common shares outstanding. This indicates profitability and desirability of a company's stock.

Objective 5. Compute and explain leverage measures.

Leverage measures indicate the extent to which a business is financed by debt and its ability to meet those debt obligations. The **debt-to-equity ratio** is total liabilities divided by total stockholders' equity. It measures the extent of overall leverage, or the proportion of borrowed capital to stockholders' equity. The **assets-to-equity ratio** offers a measure of leverage by focusing on the use of other peoples' money to acquire assets. The **times interest earned ratio** is net income (before taxes and interest) divided by interest expense. This reveals the amount of earnings (before interest and taxes) in relation to the interest requirements.

Objective 6. Explain the components of ROA and ROE.

ROA is often broken down into two components: the profit margin ratio and asset turnover to offer a better understanding of how a company generates profits. Some businesses, like supermarkets, have very low profit margin ratios, but quite high asset turnover. Others, like those in heavy manufacturing, have high profit margin ratios and low asset turnover.

ROE adds leverage, assets-to-equity, as a third component. This provides a clear indication of the extent to which a company is using borrowed money to finance the acquisition of assets. Further, it indicates the extent to which earnings available to common stockholders is enhanced through the use of debt.

Objective 7. Compute and explain market measures.

Market measures use stock market prices to offer evidence of how the company is viewed by investors. The **price-earnings ratio (PE ratio)** is often used by analysts and frequently cited on financial programs. It is computed by dividing the company's market price per share of common stock by the earnings per share of common stock. In general, a higher PE ratio suggests that investors have more confidence in a company's future earnings and growth than for a company with a low PE ratio. **Book value per share of common stock** is the total common stockholders' equity divided by common shares outstanding at year-end. Market values are not used in these calculations. However, the market value of the common stock is often compared with its book value when attempting to determine whether the stock is valued properly.

Objective 8. Explain the limitations of financial statement analysis.

The financial statements provide much meaningful information for measuring performance. However, there are other aspects of a business that are not revealed by financial statement analysis, such as customer satisfaction and morale of employees. Another limitation of analysis is that some reported data are based on approximations. Also, a two-year period of time is not conclusive evidence of a long-term trend. Comparison with other companies must be done carefully because different accounting methods may skew results. Finally, ratios involve two numbers and a change in either will affect the result. Financial statement analysis must be used with good judgment and perception.

REVIEW QUESTIONS

Instructions: Analyze each of the following items carefully before writing your answer in the column at the right.

	Question	Answer
LO 1	1. The ability to pay debts when they become due is called _______.	____________
LO 1	2. The efficiency with which assets are used to generate profits is captured with ____________ measures.	____________
LO 1	3. The ability to earn a satisfactory return on investments is called ________.	____________

LO 1 4. ________ is the proportion of debt used to operate. .... ____________________

LO 1 5. ________ measures include the PE ratio. .... ____________________

LO 1 6. A comparison of the amounts for the same line item in financial statements for two or more periods is called ________ analysis. ____________________

LO 1 7. ________ analysis reports each financial statement amount as a percentage of a designated total. .... ____________________

LO 2 8. The excess of a company's current assets over its current liabilities is called ________. .... ____________________

LO 2 9. The ________ ratio is calculated by dividing current assets by current liabilities. .... ____________________

LO 2 10. The quick or ________ ratio is calculated by dividing quick assets by ________. .... ____________________

____

LO 3 11. Accounts receivable turnover is calculated by dividing ________ on account by average accounts receivable. .... ____________________

LO 3 12. Merchandise inventory turnover is calculated by dividing ______ by average merchandise inventory. .... ____________________

LO 4 13. The return on assets is computed by dividing ______________ by average assets. .... ____________________

LO 4 14. ________ is calculated by dividing net income available to common stockholders by average common stockholders' equity. ____________________

LO 4 15. Earnings per share of common stock is calculated by dividing net income available to common stockholders by average ________ outstanding. .... ____________________

LO 5 16. The debt-to-equity ratio is a(n) ________ measure. .... ____________________

LO 5 17. The times interest earned ratio is computed by dividing net income before taxes and interest by ________. .... ____________________

LO 7 18. A measure of the ownership equity represented by each share of common stock is known as ________. .... ____________________

EXERCISES

Exercises 1–17

Provided on page 418 are comparative financial statements for Neva Corporation. (Round all calculations to two decimal places.)

Neva Corporation
Comparative Income Statement
For Years Ended December 31, 20-2 and 20-1

	20-2	20-1
Net sales (all on account)	$1,399,352	$1,308,640
Cost of goods sold	757,667	708,030
Gross profit	$ 641,685	$ 600,610
Operating expenses	480,191	435,307
Operating income	$ 161,494	$ 165,303
Other revenues and expenses	(20,036)	(20,796)
Income before income tax	$ 141,458	$ 144,507
Income tax expense	10,365	11,250
Net income	$ 131,093	$ 133,257

Neva Corporation
Comparative Balance Sheet
December 31, 20-2 and 20-1

	20-2	20-1
Assets		
Current assets:		
Cash	$ 49,646	$ 41,904
Government notes	20,000	15,000
Accounts receivable (net)	75,000	64,500
Merchandise inventory	106,650	106,150
Supplies and prepayments	9,422	13,221
Total current assets	$ 260,718	$ 240,775
Property, plant, and equipment:		
Land	$ 250,000	$ 175,000
Building (net)	480,000	520,000
Delivery equipment (net)	50,000	55,000
Office equipment (net)	35,000	27,500
Patents	10,000	12,000
Total property, plant, and equipment	$ 825,000	$ 789,500
Total assets	$1,085,718	$1,030,275
Liabilities		
Current liabilities:		
Notes payable	$ 30,000	$ 25,000
Accounts payable	78,500	95,600
Accrued and withheld payroll tax	6,200	5,600
Accrued interest payable	2,050	1,700
Total current liabilities	$ 116,750	$ 127,900
Long-term liabilities:		
Bonds payable	200,000	225,000
Total liabilities	$ 316,750	$ 352,900
Stockholders' Equity		
Common stock ($10 par)	$ 250,000	$ 200,000
Paid-in capital in excess of par	158,500	138,000
Retained earnings	360,468	339,375
Total stockholders' equity	$ 768,968	$ 677,375
Total liabilities and stockholders' equity	$1,085,718	$1,030,275

Exercise 1 (LO 2) COMPUTE WORKING CAPITAL

Compute the working capital on December 31, 20-2 and 20-1.

Exercise 2 (LO 2) COMPUTE THE CURRENT RATIO

Compute the current ratio on December 31, 20-2 and 20-1.

Exercise 3 (LO 2) COMPUTE THE QUICK OR ACID-TEST RATIO

Compute the quick or acid-test ratio on December 31, 20-2 and 20-1.

Exercise 4 (LO 3) COMPUTE THE ACCOUNTS RECEIVABLE TURNOVER

Compute the accounts receivable turnover and the average number of days the receivables were on the books for 20-2.

Exercise 5 (LO 3) COMPUTE THE MERCHANDISE INVENTORY TURNOVER

Compute the merchandise inventory turnover and the average number of days the merchandise inventory was held during 20-2.

Exercise 6 (LO 3) COMPUTE THE ASSET TURNOVER

Compute the asset turnover for 20-2.

Exercise 7 (LO 4) COMPUTE THE PROFIT MARGIN RATIO

Compute the profit margin ratio for 20-2.

Exercise 8 (LO 4) COMPUTE THE RETURN ON ASSETS

Compute the return on assets for 20-2.

Exercise 9 (LO 4) COMPUTE THE RETURN ON COMMON STOCKHOLDERS' EQUITY

Compute the return on common stockholders' equity for 20-2.

Exercise 10 (LO 4) COMPUTE EARNINGS PER SHARE OF COMMON STOCK

Compute earnings per share of common stock for 20-2. (Neva issued 5,000 shares of common stock in the middle of 20-2.)

Exercise 11 (LO 5) COMPUTE THE DEBT-TO-EQUITY RATIO

Compute the debt-to-equity ratio for December 31, 20-2.

Exercise 12 (LO 5) COMPUTE THE ASSETS-TO-EQUITY RATIO

Compute the assets-to-equity ratio on December 31, 20-2.

Exercise 13 (LO 5) COMPUTE THE TIMES INTEREST EARNED RATIO

Compute the times interest earned ratio for 20-2. Assume interest expense for 20-2 was $22,250.

Exercise 14 (LO 6) COMPUTE RETURN ON ASSETS (ROA) USING THE TWO PRIMARY COMPONENTS

Compute the return on assets (ROA) using the two primary components for 20-2 (round all calculations to two decimal places).

Exercise 15 (LO 6) COMPUTE RETURN ON COMMON STOCKHOLDERS' EQUITY (ROE) USING THE THREE PRIMARY COMPONENTS

Compute the return on common stockholders' equity (ROE) using the three primary components for 20-2 (round all calculations to two decimal places).

Exercise 16 (LO 7) COMPUTE THE PRICE-EARNINGS RATIO (PE)

Compute the price-earnings ratio (PE ratio) on December 31, 20-2. The market value of the common stock was $116.00 per share.

Exercise 17 (LO 7) COMPUTE THE BOOK VALUE PER SHARE OF COMMON STOCK

Compute the book value per share of common stock on December 31, 20-2.

PROBLEMS

Problem 18 (LO 1) HORIZONTAL ANALYSIS OF AN INCOME STATEMENT

A comparative income statement for Ala Moana Company for the last two years is started below.

Required:

Complete the statement, showing horizontal analysis by entering the amount of increase (decrease) and the percentage change for each item reported. (Round to one decimal place.)

Ala Moana Company

Comparative Income Statement

For Years Ended December 31, 20-2 and 20-1

	20-2	20-1	INCREASE (DECREASE)	PERCENT
Net sales	$971,772	$908,778		
Cost of goods sold	547,690	517,968		
Gross profit	$424,082	$390,810		
Operating expenses	396,675	347,890		
Operating income	$ 27,407	$ 42,920		
Other revenues and expenses	(1,000)	(2,000)		
Income before income tax	$ 26,407	$ 40,920		
Income tax expense	7,922	13,504		
Net income	$ 18,485	$ 27,416		

Problem 19 (LO 1) VERTICAL ANALYSIS OF AN INCOME STATEMENT

Refer to Problem 18.

Required:

Prepare a comparative income statement for Ala Moana Company, showing vertical analysis. (Round to one decimal place.)

	20-2	PERCENT	20-1	PERCENT

Problem 20 (LO 1) HORIZONTAL ANALYSIS OF A BALANCE SHEET

A comparative balance sheet for Ala Moana Company is started below.

Required:

Complete the condensed comparative balance sheet, showing horizontal analysis. (Round to one decimal place.)

Ala Moana Company

Comparative Balance Sheet

December 31, 20-2 and 20-1

	20-2	20-1	INCREASE (DECREASE)	PERCENT
Assets				
Current assets	$179,318	$167,204		
Property, plant, and equipment:				
Land	$130,000	$130,000		
Building (net)	400,000	450,000		
Delivery equipment (net)	30,000	39,000		
Office equipment (net)	47,800	51,600		
Patents	8,000	9,000		
Total property, plant, and equip.	$615,800	$679,600		
Total assets	$795,118	$846,804		
Liabilities				
Current liabilities	$ 86,675	$121,165		
Long-term liabilities:				
Bonds payable	300,000	350,000		
Total liabilities	$386,675	$471,165		
Stockholders' Equity				
Common stock	$215,000	$200,000		
Paid-in capital in excess of par	125,000	120,000		
Retained earnings	68,443	55,639		
Total stockholders' equity	$408,443	$375,639		
Total liab. and stockholders' equity	$795,118	$846,804		

Problem 21 (LO 1) VERTICAL ANALYSIS OF A BALANCE SHEET

Refer to Problem 20.

Required:

Prepare a comparative balance sheet for Ala Moana Company, showing vertical analysis. (Round to one decimal place.)

	20-2	PERCENT	20-1	PERCENT

CHAPTER 25
DEPARTMENTAL ACCOUNTING

LEARNING OBJECTIVES

Chapter 25 shows how a business can better manage its operations by dividing the organization into departments. Decisions affecting such things as profitability and the future operations of a department can be improved through analyzing departmental accounting reports.

Objective 1. Explain the nature and purpose of departmental accounting.

Departmental accounting provides more useful information than the typical income statement. Departmental reports are useful to management for planning, controlling, and evaluating performance. These reports are for internal management use only and are affected by whether the department is a cost center, profit center, or investment center.

Objective 2. Describe and compute departmental gross profit.

Departmental gross profit is the difference between a department's net sales and cost of goods sold. To compute departmental gross profit, the amount of each element of gross profit must be determined for each department. There are two ways of accumulating this information: (1) separate general ledger accounts can be maintained by department for each of the elements (accounts) making up gross profit, or (2) a single general ledger account can be maintained for each of the elements. The total in each account is then assigned to the appropriate departments at the end of the accounting period. Gross profit percentages can be computed by dividing each department's gross profit by its respective net sales.

Objective 3. Describe and compute departmental operating income.

Departmental operating income is the difference between a department's gross profit and its operating expenses. To compute departmental operating income, the elements of gross profit and the operating expenses must be determined for each department. As with departmental gross profit, there are two ways of accumulating operating expense data: (1) separate general ledger departmental operating expense accounts can be used, or (2) a single general ledger account can be maintained for each operating expense. The total in each account is then assigned or allocated to appropriate departments at the end of the accounting period.

Direct expenses are operating expenses incurred for the sole benefit of and traceable directly to a specific department. **Indirect expenses** are operating expenses incurred for the benefit of the business as a whole. These expenses cannot be traced directly to a specific department. In computing departmental operating income, direct expenses are assigned to departments based on the actual expenses incurred. Indirect expenses are allocated to departments on some reasonable basis, such as relative sales.

A **departmental operating expense summary** is a useful way to summarize the assignment and allocation of departmental operating expenses. This summary shows the following: (1) classification of each operating expense as direct or indirect, (2) amount assigned or allocated to each department, and (3) total operating expenses for each department.

Objective 4. Describe and compute departmental direct operating margin.

Departmental direct operating margin is the difference between a department's gross profit and its direct operating expenses. To compute departmental direct operating margin, the elements of gross profit and the direct operating expenses are needed for each department.

The direct operating margin can be used by management in the following ways:

1. To evaluate department performance.
2. To determine the contribution a department makes to the overall operating income of the company.
3. To decide whether to discontinue a department.

REVIEW QUESTIONS

Instructions: Analyze each of the following items carefully before writing your answer in the column at the right.

		Question	**Answer**
LO 1	**1.**	In what three ways are departmental reports useful to management?	________________ ________________ ________________
LO 1	2.	A department that incurs costs and generates revenue is called a	________________
LO 2	**3.**	The difference between a department's net sales and cost of goods sold is called ________.	________________
LO 2	**4.**	Gross profit divided by net sales is called the ________.	________________
LO 3	**5.**	The difference between a department's gross profit and its operating expenses is called ________.	________________
LO 3	**6.**	Departmental operating expenses are either direct or ________.	________________
LO 3	**7.**	Operating expenses incurred for the sole benefit of and traceable directly to a specific department are called ________.	________________
LO 3	**8.**	Operating expenses incurred for the benefit of the business as a whole and untraceable directly to a specific department are called ________.	________________
LO 3	**9.**	In the text, the base used to allocate Store Clerks' Wages Expense and Advertising Expense is the ________.	________________
LO 3	**10.**	In the text, the base used to allocate Store Rent Expense is the ________.	________________
LO 3	**11.**	In the text, Bad Debt Expense is assigned to departments based on ________.	________________
LO 4	**12.**	The difference between a department's gross profit and its direct operating expenses is called ________.	________________

EXERCISES

Exercise 1 (LO 2) DEPARTMENTAL GROSS PROFIT SECTION AND GROSS PROFIT PERCENTAGE

Selected data for Pittsfield Plumbing and Hardware Supplies are provided below. Prepare a condensed income statement reporting gross profit for each department and in total for the year ended December 31, 20--. Compute the gross profit percentage for each department. [Round calculations to the nearest percent.]

Net sales—plumbing supplies	$100,550
Net sales—hardware	250,000
Cost of goods sold—plumbing supplies	70,480
Cost of goods sold—hardware	155,870
Operating expenses	95,700

	Plumbing Supplies	Hardware	Total

Exercise 2 (LO 3) ALLOCATING OPERATING EXPENSES ON DIFFERENT BASES

Miller and Hastey are partners engaged in selling floor and wall covering. They keep accounts and prepare reports on a departmental basis. Using the data listed below, determine the amount of each expense to be assigned and allocated to each department for the year ended December 31, 20--. Identify both direct and indirect expenses [Round calculations to the nearest percent.]

1. Store clerk wages. Wages requiring allocation are distributed to the departments on the basis of relative net sales. Net sales for each department are as follows:

Net sales—wall covering	$485,000
Net sales—floor covering	538,866

Employee No.	Dept.	Wages
1	Floor	$ 25,800
2	Wall	22,600
3	Floor	28,988
4	Both	31,800
5	Both	18,640
Total		$127,828

2. Miller & Hastey has four installers who maintain records of the amount of time spent on installation for each department. Wages for each employee for the year are assigned to each department based on the hours reported.

Employee No.	Hours—Floor	Hours—Wall	Total Wages
8	1,288	658	$21,406
9	1,180	850	23,345
10	980	1,480	30,258
11	300	1,725	19,743

3. Miller & Hastey rents a store to display samples of its floor and wall coverings and to store the merchandise. Rent for the year was $9,900. This expense is assigned to each department based on the square footage used by each department.

Department	Square Footage
Floor	4,280 sq. ft.
Wall	2,600 sq. ft.

Exercise 2 (Continued)

Allocation of Expenses to Departments

Expense	Department	Direct	Indirect	Total
1.				
2.				
3.				

Calculations

1. ______________________________

Exercise 2 (Continued)

2.

Exercise 2 (Concluded)

3. ____

Exercise 3 (LO 3) DEPARTMENTAL OPERATING EXPENSE SUMMARY

Based on the information in Exercise 2, prepare a departmental operating expense summary.

Miller & Hastey
Departmental Operating Expense Summary
For Year Ended December 31, 20--

		Floor Covering			Wall Covering		
Expense	Total	Direct	Indirect	Total	Direct	Indirect	Total

PROBLEMS

Problem 4 (LO 2/3) INCOME STATEMENT WITH DEPARTMENTAL GROSS PROFIT AND OPERATING INCOME

Moss and Miller Bakery Shop reports the following summary of operating expenses for the year ended December 31, 20--:

Moss and Miller Bakery Shop
Departmental Operating Expense Summary
For Year Ended December 31, 20--

	Cake Department	Bread Department	Total
Bakery wages expense	$ 45,600	$ 82,800	$128,400
Truck drivers' wages expense	23,800	38,800	62,600
Depreciation expense—delivery equipment	12,600	11,400	24,000
Bakery rent expense	10,700	15,800	26,500
Bad debt expense	2,300	1,800	4,100
Other operating expenses	128,200	95,600	223,800
	$223,200	$246,200	$469,400

Net sales and cost of goods sold for the year were as follows:

	Cake Department	Bread Department
Net sales	$850,000	$770,000
Cost of goods sold	488,500	526,800

Required:

Prepare a condensed income statement showing departmental gross profits and operating income.

	Cake Dept.	Bread Dept.	Total

Problem 5 (LO 2/3) INCOME STATEMENT WITH DEPARTMENTAL OPERATING INCOME AND TOTAL OPERATING INCOME

Bill Hickock owns a business called Wild West Wear. He has divided his business into two departments: boots and accessories. The information provided below is for the fiscal year ended June 30, 20--.

	Boots	Accessories
Net sales	$550,200	$257,000
Cost of goods sold	247,600	141,400
Wages expense	107,000	50,800
Advertising expense	43,200	15,700
Other operating expenses	49,000	26,000

Required:

1. Prepare an income statement showing departmental operating income and total operating income.
2. Calculate departmental operating expense and operating income percentages. [Round calculations to one decimal place.]

1.

	Boots	Accessories	Total

Problem 5 (Concluded)

2.

Problem 6 (LO 2/3/4) INCOME STATEMENT WITH DEPARTMENTAL DIRECT OPERATING MARGIN AND TOTAL OPERATING INCOME

Joyce Kennington operates a business called Games Unlimited that sells video games, pinball machines, and pocket billiards for home and commercial use. The following information is provided for the year ended December 31, 20--:

	Home Market	Commercial Market
Net sales	$284,000	$395,000
Cost of goods sold	146,250	175,000
Direct operating expenses:		
Advertising expense	$ 26,000	$ 38,000
Store clerks' wages expense	32,000	36,000
Truck drivers' wages expense	13,000	16,000
Bad debt expense	5,000	7,000
Depreciation expense—delivery equipment	8,000	6,000
Other operating expenses	24,000	18,000
Indirect operating expenses:		
Store clerks' wages expense	$ 12,000	
Advertising expense	11,000	
Store rent expense	22,000	
Other operating expenses	15,000	

Required:

1. Prepare an income statement showing departmental direct operating margin and total operating income, using the form on the following page.
2. Calculate departmental direct operating margin percentages in the space provided below. [Round calculations to one decimal place.]

2.

Problem 6 (Concluded)

1.

	Home Market	Commercial Market	Total

Problem 7 (LO 4) WHETHER TO DISCONTINUE A DEPARTMENT

Jones and Abdel are reviewing the operating activities of their four departments for the current year as follows:

	Dept. A	Dept. B	Dept. C	Dept. D	Total
Net sales	$550,000	$480,000	$625,000	$340,000	$1,995,000
Cost of goods sold	385,000	288,000	468,750	170,000	1,311,750
Gross profit	$165,000	$192,000	$156,250	$170,000	$ 683,250
Direct operating expenses	95,000	108,000	78,000	190,000	471,000
Direct operating margin	$ 70,000	$ 84,000	$ 78,250	$(20,000)	$ 212,250
Indirect operating expenses	78,000	45,000	36,000	13,000	172,000
Operating income (loss)	$ (8,000)	$ 39,000	$ 42,250	$(33,000)	$ 40,250

Required:

Determine whether any of the departments should be eliminated. Explain.

CHAPTER 26
MANUFACTURING ACCOUNTING: THE JOB ORDER COST SYSTEM

LEARNING OBJECTIVES

Chapter 26 introduces the manufacturing business, as contrasted with a service or merchandising business. The major difference lies in the asset account called Inventory. In a manufacturing business, there are three inventory accounts—Materials, Work in Process, and Finished Goods. As a result, financial statements are prepared slightly differently, and costs are accumulated differently in a job order cost accounting system.

Objective 1. Describe the three manufacturing costs.

The three costs incurred to manufacture a product are materials, labor, and factory overhead. **Materials** include both direct materials (those that are a major part of the finished product) and indirect materials (those that are used in the manufacturing process but are a minor part of the finished product). **Labor** is also direct and indirect. **Factory overhead** includes the indirect manufacturing costs, including indirect materials, indirect labor, and other factory overhead (such as depreciation, repairs, insurance, and taxes on the factory and equipment).

Objective 2. Describe the three inventories of a manufacturing business.

Materials inventory consists of all materials used to produce the final product, including both direct and indirect materials.

Work in process inventory includes all products on which work has begun but is not finished at the end of the accounting period. The cost of work in process inventory includes materials, labor, and factory overhead.

Finished goods inventory contains the costs of finished products that are ready for sale.

Objective 3. Describe and illustrate how manufacturing costs and inventories affect the financial statements of a manufacturing business.

The main difference between manufacturing and merchandising company income statements is that cost of goods manufactured on the manufacturer's income statement replaces purchases on the merchandiser's income statement. In addition, the cost of goods sold section of the manufacturer's income statement is supplemented by a schedule of cost of goods manufactured. This schedule lists the amount of beginning work in process; materials, labor, and factory overhead added to production; ending work in process; and cost of goods manufactured during the accounting period.

The balance sheet is also slightly different. In the current assets section, a manufacturing business lists three inventories: finished goods, work in process, and materials. The merchandising business lists only merchandise inventory.

Objective 4. Define and describe how to operate a job order cost accounting system.

A **job order cost system** provides a separate record of the cost of producing each individual product or group of products. A perpetual inventory system is used to maintain a continuous record of the flow of costs through the manufacturing inventory accounts. Journal entries are required to recognize that (1) materials are purchased, (2) materials are issued to production, (3) product is completed, and (4) completed product is sold.

A record of materials is kept in a materials ledger or stores ledger. Materials requisitions are used to issue materials from the storeroom to production. Employee earnings are recorded on time sheets, and direct labor costs are charged to work in process. Indirect labor costs are charged to factory overhead.

Factory overhead consists of indirect materials, indirect labor, and all other indirect manufacturing costs. These actual factory overhead costs are accumulated in the factory overhead account and in a factory overhead subsidiary ledger. Using a factory overhead control account, a reasonable amount of factory overhead is assigned to specific job orders, even though all costs may not be known at the time the product is finished. This is called applying factory overhead using a **predetermined overhead rate**. The rate is calculated by dividing estimated total factory overhead costs by some measure of production activity—usually direct labor hours, direct labor costs, or machine hours.

All direct materials, direct labor, and factory overhead costs applied on each job are accumulated on a job cost sheet. After a job is completed, all costs accumulated on the job cost sheet are transferred to Finished Goods.

Generally, factory overhead applied will not be exactly the same amount as the actual overhead accumulated in the factory overhead account. The difference is called **overapplied** or **underapplied overhead**. Unless the amount is large, this balance usually is transferred to the cost of goods sold account at the end of the accounting period by an adjusting entry.

Objective 5. Describe a process cost accounting system.

Rather than using job orders to record a product's cost, a manufacturer may elect to use a **process cost system**. As a product flows through the manufacturing process, costs are attached and passed along at each point or process of production. For example, costs in the cutting department would be applied to the product before it entered the finishing department.

REVIEW QUESTIONS

Instructions: Analyze each of the following items carefully before writing your answer in the column at the right.

	Question	Answer
LO 1	**1.** The three costs incurred to manufacture a product are ________, ________, and ________.	________________ ________________ ________________
LO 1	**2.** Materials that enter into and become a major part of a finished product are called ________ materials.	________________
LO 1	**3.** Materials used in production that do not become a major part of a finished product are called ________ materials.	________________
LO 1	**4.** Wages of employees directly involved with converting materials into finished goods are called ________ labor.	________________
LO 1	**5.** Wages and salaries of people not directly involved with production are called ________ labor.	________________
LO 1	**6.** All manufacturing costs, other than direct materials and direct labor, are called ________.	________________

LO 1 7. The three major components of factory overhead are ________, ________, and ________. .... ________________ ________________ ________________

LO 2 8. Three major inventories of a manufacturing business are ________, ________, and ________. .... ________________ ________________ ________________

LO 2 9. Work in process inventory consists of three main components: ________, ________, and ________. .... ________________ ________________ ________________

LO 3 10. A merchandising company adds purchases to beginning inventory to calculate goods available for sale; a manufacturing company adds ________ to beginning inventory. .... ________________

LO 3 11. The balance sheet of a manufacturing company includes three inventory accounts: ________, ________, and ________. ...... ________________ ________________ ________________

LO 4 12. A(n) ________ cost system provides a separate record of the cost of each product or group of products that is produced. ...... ________________

LO 4 13. When raw materials are purchased, the cost is debited to an inventory account called ________. .... ________________

LO 4 14. The materials account in the general ledger is a control account; a separate account for each type of material is kept in a(n) ________ ledger, called a materials or stores ledger. .... ________________

LO 4 15. Materials are issued from the storeroom to production based on a form called the ________. .... ________________

LO 4 16. Direct labor is debited to the ________ inventory account. ...... ________________

LO 4 17. The factory overhead account is a control account; details are accumulated in the factory overhead ________ ledger. .... ________________

LO 4 18. When factory overhead costs are applied to specific jobs, they are applied based on a(n) ________ rate. .... ________________

LO 4 19. A(n) ________ sheet is a document for recording the direct materials, direct labor, and factory overhead costs incurred on a specific job. .... ____________________

LO 4 20. Finished Goods is a(n) ________ account in the general ledger. A separate account for each product is kept in a finished goods ledger. .... ____________________

LO 4 21. If the amount of applied overhead is greater than the actual overhead cost incurred, the difference is called ________ overhead. .... ____________________

LO 4 22. If the amount of applied overhead is less than actual overhead cost incurred, the difference is called ________ overhead. .... ____________________

LO 5 23. A(n) ________ cost system accumulates manufacturing costs by process; each unit passing through the process is assigned a share of the costs. .... ____________________

LO 5 24. A(n) ________ cost system is useful for costing similar or identical products. .... ____________________

EXERCISES

Exercise 1 (LO 3) SCHEDULE OF COST OF GOODS MANUFACTURED

Prepare a schedule of cost of goods manufactured for Jonas Manufacturing Company, based on the following information: (Assume that all materials inventory items are direct materials.)

Work in process, January 1, 20--	$22,000
Materials inventory, January 1, 20--	18,000
Materials purchases	19,000
Materials inventory, December 31, 20--	21,500
Direct labor	16,500
Factory overhead	8,200
Work in process, December 31, 20--	24,000

Exercise 2 (LO 3) COST OF GOODS SOLD SECTION

Prepare a cost of goods sold section of the income statement for Jonas Manufacturing Company, using the schedule of cost of goods manufactured from Exercise 1 and the following information:

Finished goods inventory, January 1, 20--	$28,000
Finished goods inventory, December 31, 20--	26,000

Exercise 3 (LO 3) CURRENT ASSETS SECTION OF BALANCE SHEET

Prepare the current assets section of a balance sheet for Jonas Manufacturing Company, using information from Exercises 1 and 2 (for inventory balances) and the following information:

Cash	$18,000
Accounts receivable	15,000
Supplies	8,000

Exercise 4 (LO 4) JOB ORDER COST SHEET

Below is a job order cost sheet for Job No. 329. From the daily time sheet, post direct labor to the cost sheet; from the materials requisition, post direct materials to the job cost sheet. Factory overhead is applied as a percentage of direct labor costs (50%). Complete the job cost sheet from the information supplied.

WATERTOWN
Manufacturing Co.

JOB COST SHEET

Job No. 329 Date Started Jan. 24, 20--

Item RC Boat

For Lakeside Wholesalers Date Completed Feb. 22, 20--

DIRECT MATERIALS		DIRECT LABOR		FACTORY OVERHEAD	
Req. No.	Amount	Hours	Amount	Direct Labor	
471	$600	301	$1,000	Overhead Rate	
				Overhead Applied	
				SUMMARY	
				Direct Materials	
				Direct Labor	
				Overhead	
				Total Cost	

Exercise 4 (Concluded)

WATERTOWN
Manufacturing Co.

DAILY TIME SHEET

Name Charles Shirley Date Feb. 4, 20--

Job No.	Start	Stop	Hours Reg.	Hours O.T.	Equiv. Hours	Rate	Amount Earned
329	8:00	12:00	4		4	10.00	$40.00
329	1:00	6:00	4	1	5 1/2	10.00	55.00
							$95.00

MATERIALS REQUISITION

Requested Susan Rosman Req. No. 507

Date: January 29, 20-- Approved: C.D.

Charge to: Job No. 329—Materials

Item No.	Description	Quantity	Unit Cost	Total Cost
PT10	16" Plastic Boat Body	1,000	1.50	$1,500

Received by: S.R. *Date Received:* January 29, 20--

Exercise 5 (LO 4) PREDETERMINED FACTORY OVERHEAD RATE

Based on the following information, compute the predetermined overhead application rate based on (a) direct labor hours, (b) direct labor costs, and (c) machine hours.

Total estimated factory overhead costs	$600,000
Total estimated direct labor hours	100,000
Total estimated direct labor costs	$400,000
Total estimated machine hours	200,000

Exercise 6 (LO 4) APPLICATION OF FACTORY OVERHEAD

Using the rates calculated in Exercise 5, determine the overhead applied to the following jobs, based on (a) direct labor hours, (b) direct labor costs, and (c) machine hours.

1. Job No. 101: 10 direct labor hours
   $80 direct labor costs
   30 machine hours
2. Job No. 102: 25 direct labor hours
   $250 direct labor costs
   60 machine hours
3. Job No. 103: 15 direct labor hours
   $100 direct labor costs
   12 machine hours

PROBLEMS

Problem 7 (LO 4) JOURNAL ENTRIES FOR MATERIAL, LABOR, AND OVERHEAD

Required:

Based on the following information, prepare general journal entries for Aztel Manufacturing Company. Label the entries (a) through (j).

(a) Purchased raw materials on account, $28,000.
(b) Issued direct materials to production, $12,000. Job No. 101.
Issued direct materials to production, $10,000. Job No. 102.
(c) Issued indirect materials to production, $4,000.
(d) Allocated payroll, direct labor to production, $13,000. Job No. 101.
Allocated payroll, direct labor to production, $11,000. Job No. 102.
(e) Allocated indirect labor costs to production, $2,500.
(f) Paid miscellaneous factory overhead charges, $5,000.
(g) Allocated factory overhead to Job Nos. 101 and 102 based on a predetermined factory overhead rate of 50% of direct labor costs.
(h) Finished Job Nos. 101 and 102 and transferred them to finished goods as products A and B.
(i) Sold products A and B for $35,000 and $29,000, respectively.
(j) Transferred the balance in the factory overhead account to Cost of Goods Sold (under- or overapplied factory overhead).

GENERAL JOURNAL

PAGE

	DATE	DESCRIPTION	POST. REF.	DEBIT	CREDIT	
1						1
2						2
3						3
4						4
5						5
6						6
7						7
8						8
9						9
10						10
11						11
12						12
13						13
14						14
15						15
16						16
17						17
18						18
19						19
20						20

Name ____________________

Problem 7 (Concluded)

GENERAL JOURNAL

PAGE

DATE		DESCRIPTION	POST. REF.	DEBIT	CREDIT

Problem 8 (LO 4) JOURNAL ENTRIES FOR MATERIAL, LABOR, OVERHEAD, AND SALES

Required:

Based on the following information, prepare general journal entries for B. R. Campbell Company. Using a general journal, label the entries (a) through (j). Calculate the predetermined factory overhead rate, based on total estimated factory overhead of $15,000 and anticipated total direct labor hours of 7,500. Post the transactions to the following T accounts: Materials, Work in Process (subsidiary ledger accounts for Job Nos. 20–23), Finished Goods, Cost of Goods Sold, and Factory Overhead.

(a) Purchased materials on account, $40,000.

(b) Direct materials requisitioned to production:

Job No. 20	$10,000
Job No. 21	8,000
Job No. 22	7,000
Job No. 23	9,000

(c) Indirect materials requisitioned to production, $1,000.

(d) Direct labor charged to production:

Job No. 20: 125 direct labor hours	$1,500
Job No. 21: 300 direct labor hours	3,200
Job No. 22: 175 direct labor hours	2,000
Job No. 23: 250 direct labor hours	3,000

(e) Indirect labor charged to production, $500.

(f) Other miscellaneous factory overhead charges paid, $300.

(g) Factory overhead applied is charged to Job Nos. 20–23 based on the predetermined factory overhead rate.

(h) Job Nos. 20–23 are finished and transferred to finished goods as products D, E, F, and G.

(i) Products D, E, F, and G are sold for $13,000, $12,800, $10,700, and $14,300, respectively.

(j) Actual factory overhead is not the same as factory overhead applied.
Actual factory overhead: $1,800
Transfer the difference (under- or overapplied factory overhead) to Cost of Goods Sold.

Problem 8 (Continued)

GENERAL JOURNAL

PAGE

DATE		DESCRIPTION	POST. REF.	DEBIT	CREDIT

Problem 8 (Continued)

GENERAL JOURNAL

PAGE

DATE		DESCRIPTION	POST. REF.	DEBIT	CREDIT

Problem 8 (Concluded)

Materials	

Work in Process: Job No. 20	

Work in Process: Job No. 21	

Work in Process: Job No. 22	

Work in Process: Job No. 23	

Finished Goods	

Cost of Goods Sold	

Factory Overhead	

CHAPTER 27
ADJUSTMENTS, FINANCIAL STATEMENTS, AND YEAR-END ACCOUNTING FOR A MANUFACTURING BUSINESS

LEARNING OBJECTIVES

Chapter 27 shows how to use the spreadsheet to prepare the end-of-period adjustments and the financial statements of a manufacturing company. Both the spreadsheet and financial statements of a manufacturing company differ from those of a merchandising company.

Objective 1. Prepare a 6-column spreadsheet for a manufacturing company.

The spreadsheet for a manufacturing company is similar to the one illustrated in Chapter 14 for a merchandising company. The same four steps applied in Chapter 14 are used to prepare this spreadsheet.

1. Prepare the trial balance.
2. Prepare the adjustments.
3. Prepare the adjusted trial balance.
4. Add all of the income statement accounts listed in the adjusted trial balance columns to compute the net income (loss) for the period.

Unlike a merchandising company that uses a single inventory, a manufacturing company has three inventories:

1. finished goods
2. work in process, and
3. materials.

All three of these inventories appear on the balance sheet and are classified as current assets.

A manufacturer uses a perpetual inventory system, so that the movement of goods from Materials to Work in Process to Finished Goods to Cost of Goods Sold is recorded as the movement occurs. For example, each time finished goods are sold, Cost of Goods Sold is debited and Finished Goods Inventory is credited for the cost of the goods sold. If there is a difference between the physical count and the amount in the perpetual inventory records, an adjusting entry is needed to correct the records.

Factory Overhead includes all costs of manufacturing a product that are not either direct materials or direct labor. Both the debit and credit balances of Factory Overhead appear in the adjusted trial balance columns on the spreadsheet. The debit balance represents actual overhead costs incurred. The credit balance represents factory overhead applied to production.

Objective 2. Prepare adjustments to (1) apply factory overhead to ending work in process, (2) record additional actual factory overhead, (3) record under- or overapplied overhead, (4) record expected sales returns and allowances, (5) record other expenses not involving overhead, and (6) provide for corporate income taxes.

Many adjustments on the spreadsheet are similar to those illustrated in Chapter 14. The new ones for a manufacturing company are summarized as follows:

(1) Factory overhead is applied to jobs not completed at the end of the year to properly value the ending work in process inventory. This is done by debiting Work in Process and crediting Factory Overhead.

(2) Factory supplies and insurance related to the factory and to factory equipment must be adjusted at year-end. These adjustments involve a debit to Factory Overhead and a credit to Factory Supplies and Prepaid

Insurance. Depreciation on the factory building and factory equipment is recorded by debiting Factory Overhead and crediting the related accumulated depreciation accounts.

(3) At the end of the year, the factory overhead account is examined. If the debit side is larger than the credit side, this indicates underapplied overhead. This underapplied overhead is closed into Cost of Goods Sold. If the credit side of Factory Overhead is larger than the debit side, this indicates overapplied overhead. This overapplied overhead is closed into Cost of Goods Sold.

Adjustments also are made for expected sales returns and allowances and for three expenses not involving overhead: interest on bonds payable, uncollectible accounts, and depreciation on the office equipment.

An adjustment to corporate income tax is necessary because the amount of estimated income tax paid during the year does not equal the actual amount of income tax owed.

The spreadsheet is completed by extending the amounts to the adjusted trial balance columns. The debit and credit factory overhead account balances are extended and will be used in the process of closing the accounts.

Objective 3. Prepare financial statements for a manufacturing company.

Financial statements prepared for a manufacturing company include an income statement, statement of retained earnings, balance sheet, and statement of cash flows. The statement of cash flows is essentially the same in format as the one illustrated in Chapter 23, so it is not illustrated in this chapter. ToyJoy is a manufacturer, so its income statement is supported by a schedule of cost of goods manufactured. ToyJoy is a corporation, so its statement of retained earnings includes a deduction for dividends paid. As a manufacturer, ToyJoy's balance sheet includes three inventory accounts.

Objective 4. Prepare adjusting, closing, and reversing journal entries for a manufacturing company.

Each of the entries appearing in the Adjustments columns of the spreadsheet must be journalized.

The adjustment to apply factory overhead to work in process does not include any entries to the individual jobs in the job cost ledger. This is because only the aggregate work in process needs to be adjusted for financial reporting purposes at year-end. The aggregate adjustment will be reversed at the beginning of the following period.

Six steps are involved in closing the manufacturer's temporary accounts.

1. The debit "balance" in the factory overhead account is transferred to Income Summary, and the subsidiary factory overhead accounts are closed.
2. The credit "balance" in the factory overhead account is transferred to Income Summary.
3. The balances of the sales and interest revenue accounts are transferred to Income Summary.
4. The balances of Cost of Goods Sold and all expense accounts are transferred to Income Summary.
5. The balance of the income summary account is transferred to Retained Earnings.
6. The balance of the cash dividends account is transferred to Retained Earnings.

ToyJoy reverses only two adjusting entries: (1) For accrued interest on bonds payable; (2) For the application of factory overhead to Work in Process.

REVIEW QUESTIONS

Instructions: Analyze each of the following items carefully before writing your answer in the column at the right.

	Question	Answer
LO 1	**1.** In place of a single merchandise inventory account on the merchandising company spreadsheet, the three inventories for the manufacturing company are ________, ________, and ________.	______________ ______________ ______________
LO 1	**2.** Under the perpetual inventory system, ________ contains the costs recorded as sales were made during the year.	______________
LO 1	**3.** The debit side of Factory Overhead represents ________.	______________
LO 1	**4.** The credit side of Factory Overhead represents ________.	______________
LO 2	**5.** Factory overhead is applied to Work in Process at the end of the year by debiting the account ________ and crediting the account ________.	______________ ______________
LO 2	**6.** An adjustment at the end of the year to show the amount of factory supplies used includes a debit to ________.	______________
LO 2	**7.** An adjustment at the end of the year to show the amount of factory insurance expired includes a debit to ________.	______________
LO 2	**8.** An adjustment at the end of the year to show the amount of depreciation on the factory building includes a debit to ________ and a credit to ________.	______________ ______________
LO 2	**9.** At the end of the year, the factory overhead account shows the debit side is larger than the credit side. This debit balance represents (over-/under-) applied overhead.	______________
LO 2	**10.** An adjustment at the end of the year for a credit balance in the factory overhead account includes a credit to ________.	______________
LO 2	**11.** An adjustment for goods sold this year but expected to be returned next year includes a debit to Sales Returns and Allowances and a credit to ____________	______________
LO 2	**12.** An adjustment at the end of the year to show the amount of additional corporate income tax includes a credit to ________.	______________

LO 2 13. On the spreadsheet, both the debit and credit balances of the ____ account appear in the adjusted trial balance columns. .... ______________________________

____

LO 3 14. Most of the data for the income statement can be obtained from the ________ columns of the spreadsheet. .... ______________________________

LO 3 15. The main differences between a merchandising income statement and a manufacturing income statement are the ________ section and the schedule of ________. .... ______________________________

LO 3 16. Data for the balance sheet can be obtained from the adjusted trial balance columns of the spreadsheet, except for the ___________. ______________________________

____

LO 4 17. In addition to closing all revenue and expense accounts, both the debit and credit totals of the ________ account must be closed to Income Summary. .... ______________________________

LO 4 18. The closing entry for factory overhead involves a credit to Factory Overhead and a debit to ________. .... ______________________________

LO 4 19. The balance of the income summary account is transferred to ________ as part of the closing process. .... ______________________________

LO 4 20. The adjusting entry to apply factory overhead to Work in Process is reversed with a debit to ________ and a credit to ________. ______________________________

____

EXERCISES

Exercise 1 (LO 2) ADJUSTING ENTRIES INCLUDING UNDERAPPLIED/OVERAPPLIED OVERHEAD

Data for the end-of-year adjustments of Jones Company are shown below.

(a) Factory overhead is applied at a rate of 80% of direct labor costs. At the end of the year, the direct labor costs associated with the jobs still in process amounted to $10,000.

(b) Based on a physical count of factory supplies at the end of the year, it is determined that $3,525 of factory supplies were used during the year.

(c) Based on a review of the insurance policy files, it is determined that $4,295 of insurance on the factory building and equipment has expired.

(d) Depreciation expense for the year was $5,450 on the factory building and $8,735 on the factory equipment, a total of $14,185.

(e) The factory overhead account has a debit balance of $233,175 and a credit balance of $236,600 [after recording adjustments (a) through (d)].

1. Prepare adjusting journal entries as of December 31.
2. Was factory overhead under- or overapplied for the year?

1.

GENERAL JOURNAL PAGE

	DATE	DESCRIPTION	POST. REF.	DEBIT	CREDIT	
1						1
2						2
3						3
4						4
5						5
6						6
7						7
8						8
9						9
10						10
11						11
12						12
13						13
14						14
15						15
16						16
17						17
18						18

2. ______________________________

Exercise 2 (LO 3) SCHEDULE OF COST OF GOODS MANUFACTURED

Data for Brinley Company for the current fiscal year ended June 30, 20-2, are shown below.

Work in process, June 30, 20-2	$ 18,260
Materials inventory, June 30, 20-2	14,300
Materials purchased	147,150
Direct labor	290,350
Factory overhead	160,240
Work in process, July 1, 20-1	13,250
Materials inventory, July 1, 20-1	10,260
Indirect materials charged to production	4,500

Prepare a schedule of cost of goods manufactured for the year ended June 30, 20-2.

Exercise 3 (LO 2/4) ADJUSTING AND REVERSING ENTRIES

Data for the end-of-year adjustments of Dembrow Company are shown below.

Factory overhead to be applied to work in process ending inventory	$12,800
Estimate of this year's sales that will be returned next year (remaining balance from last year = $130)	770
Cost of goods expected to be returned (remaining balance from last year = $80)	510
Interest receivable	920
Provision for doubtful accounts (based on percentage of sales)	3,920
Office supplies consumed	1,350
Factory supplies consumed	4,250
Insurance expired on factory building and equipment	3,400
Depreciation—factory building	4,600
Depreciation—factory equipment	6,100
Interest payable	8,250

1. Prepare the end-of-year adjusting journal entries, as of December 31, 20-3, for Dembrow Company.
2. Prepare the reversing journal entries for Dembrow Company, as of January 2, 20-4.

Exercise 3 (Continued)

1.

GENERAL JOURNAL

PAGE

	DATE		DESCRIPTION	POST. REF.	DEBIT	CREDIT	
1							1
2							2
3							3
4							4
5							5
6							6
7							7
8							8
9							9
10							10
11							11
12							12
13							13
14							14
15							15
16							16
17							17
18							18
19							19
20							20
21							21
22							22
23							23
24							24
25							25
26							26
27							27
28							28
29							29
30							30
31							31
32							32
33							33
34							34

Exercise 3 (Concluded)

2.

GENERAL JOURNAL

PAGE

	DATE		DESCRIPTION	POST. REF.	DEBIT	CREDIT	
1							1
2							2
3							3
4							4
5							5
6							6
7							7
8							8
9							9
10							10
11							11
12							12
13							13
14							14
15							15
16							16
17							17
18							18
19							19
20							20
21							21
22							22
23							23
24							24
25							25
26							26
27							27
28							28
29							29
30							30
31							31
32							32
33							33
34							34

Exercise 4 (LO 4) CLOSING ENTRIES

Data for the closing entries of Thompson Company are shown below.

Factory overhead, debit and credit balance	$216,850
Sales	842,750
Interest revenue	1,400
Cost of goods sold	583,640
Wages expense	102,400
Office supplies expense	3,740
Depreciation expense—office equipment	6,230
Utilities expense—office	5,485
Bad debt expense	2,350
Advertising expense	9,350
Interest expense	8,420
Income tax expense	25,370
Cash dividends	16,000

Prepare closing journal entries for Thompson Company for the year ended December 31.

GENERAL JOURNAL

PAGE

	DATE		DESCRIPTION	POST. REF.	DEBIT	CREDIT	
1							1
2							2
3							3
4							4
5							5
6							6
7							7
8							8
9							9
10							10
11							11
12							12
13							13
14							14
15							15
16							16
17							17
18							18
19							19
20							20
21							21

Exercise 4 (Concluded)

GENERAL JOURNAL

PAGE

	DATE		DESCRIPTION	POST. REF.	DEBIT	CREDIT	
1							1
2							2
3							3
4							4
5							5
6							6
7							7
8							8
9							9
10							10
11							11
12							12
13							13
14							14
15							15
16							16
17							17
18							18
19							19
20							20
21							21
22							22
23							23
24							24
25							25
26							26
27							27
28							28
29							29

PROBLEMS

Problem 5 (LO 1/2/3) SPREADSHEET, ADJUSTING ENTRIES, AND FINANCIAL STATEMENTS

The trial balance portion of the spreadsheet of Rogerson Company as of December 31, 20--, is shown on pages 476 and 477.

Problem 5 (Continued)

1.

	A	B	C
1	Rogerson Company		
2	Trial Balance		
3	December 31, 20--		
4	ACCOUNT TITLE	TRIAL BALANCE	
5		DEBIT	CREDIT
6	Cash	28,300.00	
7	Government Notes	7,000.00	
8	Interest Receivable		
9	Accounts Receivable	28,000.00	
10	Allowances for Doubtful Accounts		720.00
11	Finished Goods Inventory	21,460.00	
12	Work in Process Inventory	11,320.00	
13	Materials Inventory	10,240.00	
14	Estimated Returns Inventory	50.00	
15	Office Supplies	5,720.00	
16	Factory Supplies	7,150.00	
17	Land	100,000.00	
18	Factory Building	90,000.00	
19	Accumulated Depreciation—Factory Building		15,000.00
20	Factory Equipment	50,000.00	
21	Accumulated Depreciation—Factory Equipment		10,000.00
22	Accounts Payable		15,200.00
23	Customer Refunds Payable		105.00
24	Income Tax Payable		
25	Interest Payable		
26	Bonds Payable		100,000.00
27	Capital Stock		60,000.00
28	Paid-In Capital in Excess of Par		20,000.00
29	Retained Earnings		66,215.00
30	Cash Dividends	20,000.00	
31	Sales		401,100.00
32	Sales Returns and Allowances	5,900.00	
33	Interest Revenue		500.00
34	Factory Overhead	84,600.00	97,500.00
35			
36			
37			
38	Cost of Goods Sold	210,400.00	
39			
40	Wages Expense	82,100.00	
41	Office Supplies Expense		
42	Utilities Expense—Office	5,100.00	
43	Bad Debt Expense		
44	Interest Expense	8,000.00	
45	Income Tax Expense	11,000.00	
46		786,340.00	786,340.00
47			

Problem 5 (Continued)

Data for adjusting the accounts:

(a) Factory overhead (to be applied to work in process ending inventory)	$ 2,950
(b) Estimate of this year's sales that will be returned next year	670
(c) Cost of goods expected to be returned	320
Interest accruals:	
(d) Interest receivable	100
(e) Interest payable	400
(f) Estimate of uncollectible accounts, based on an aging of accounts receivable	4,100
(g) Office supplies consumed	2,900
(h) Factory supplies consumed	4,250
Depreciation:	
(i) Factory building	3,000
(j) Factory equipment	4,500
(k) Overapplied factory overhead	4,100
(l) Provision for corporate income taxes	5,275
(m) Physical counts of the inventories agreed with amounts in the books.	

Additional data needed to prepare financial statements:

Beginning inventories:	
Finished goods, January 1	$19,300
Work in process, January 1	9,480
Materials inventory, January 1	13,650
Materials purchases for the year	43,200
Direct labor	70,290
Actual factory overhead	96,350

Assume that all materials inventory items are direct materials.

Required:

1. Complete the spreadsheet on pages 476 and 477.
2. Prepare the following financial statements and schedule:
   a. income statement on page 478.
   b. schedule of cost of goods manufactured on page 479.
   c. statement of retained earnings on page 480.
   d. balance sheet on pages 481 and 482.

Problem 5 (Continued)

2. a.

Problem 5 (Continued)

2. b.

Problem 5 (Continued)

2. c.

Problem 5 (Continued)

2. d.

Problem 5 (Concluded)

2. d.

Problem 6 (LO 1/3) FINANCIAL STATEMENTS

The adjusted trial balance columns of Omega Company's spreadsheet are shown on the next page.

Additional information needed to prepare the financial statements is as follows:

Materials inventory, January 1	$ 4,820
Work in process inventory, January 1	7,535
Finished goods inventory, January 1	20,345
Estimated returns inventory, January 1, remaining balance	65
Materials purchases	167,060
Direct labor	97,500
Actual factory overhead	104,300
Indirect materials charged to production	3,800

Required:

1. Prepare an income statement and a schedule of cost of goods manufactured for the year ended December 31, 20--.
2. Prepare a statement of retained earnings for the year ended December 31, 20--.
3. Prepare a balance sheet as of December 31, 20--.

Problem 6 (Continued)

	A	B	C
1	Omega Company		
2	Spreadsheet (Partial)		
3	For the Year Ended December 31, 20--		
4	ACCOUNT TITLE	ADJUSTED TRIAL BALANCE	
5		DEBIT	CREDIT
6	Cash	23,475.00	
7	Treasury Notes (short-term)	5,500.00	
8	Interest Receivable	95.00	
9	Accounts Receivable	48,210.00	
10	Allowances for Doubtful Accounts		2,895.00
11	Finished Goods Inventory	23,900.00	
12	Work in Process Inventory	9,845.00	
13	Materials Inventory	6,380.00	
14	Estimated Returns Inventory	530.00	
15	Office Supplies	770.00	
16	Factory Supplies	915.00	
17	Prepaid Insurance	850.00	
18	Land	30,000.00	
19	Factory Building	95,000.00	
20	Accumulated Depreciation—Factory Building		23,800.00
21	Factory Equipment	110,000.00	
22	Accumulated Depreciation—Factory Equipment		32,000.00
23	Accounts Payable		24,000.00
24	Customer Refunds Payable		330.00
25	Income Tax Payable		4,950.00
26	Interest Payable		600.00
27	Bonds Payable		60,000.00
28	Capital Stock		70,000.00
29	Paid-in Capital in Excess of Par		15,000.00
30	Retained Earnings		68,925.00
31	Cash Dividends	20,000.00	
32	Sales		541,295.00
33	Sales Returns and Allowances	7,600.00	
34	Interest Revenue		440.00
35	Factory Overhead	104,300.00	104,300.00
36			
37	Cost of Goods Sold	357,170.00	
38	Wages Expense	74,125.00	
39	Office Supplies Expense	2,500.00	
40	Utilities Expense—Office	2,200.00	
41	Bad Debt Expense	1,890.00	
42	Interest Expense	3,600.00	
43	Income Tax Expense	19,680.00	
44		948,535.00	948,535.00
45		573,065.00	646,035.00
46	Net Income	72,970.00	

Problem 6 (Continued)

1.

Problem 6 (Continued)

1.

2.

Problem 6 (Continued)

3.

Problem 6 (Concluded)

3.

Problem 7 (LO 1/2/4) Adjusting, Closing, and Reversing Entries

The completed spreadsheet of Reynolds Company as of December 31, 20-4, is shown below.

	A	B	C	D	E	F	G	H	I
1	Reynolds Company								
2	Spreadsheet								
3	For the Year Ended December 31, 20-4								
4	ACCOUNT TITLE	TRIAL BALANCE		ADJUSTMENTS				ADJUSTED TRIAL BALANCE	
5		DEBIT	CREDIT		DEBIT		CREDIT	DEBIT	CREDIT
6	Cash	34,600.00						34,600.00	
7	Government Notes	9,000.00						9,000.00	
8	Interest Receivable			(d)	165.00			165.00	
9	Accounts Receivable	23,000.00						23,000.00	
10	Allow. for Doubtful Accounts		920.00			(f)	2,475.00		3,395.00
11	Finished Goods Inventory	25,000.00						25,000.00	
12	Work in Process Inventory	12,600.00		(a)	2,850.00			15,450.00	
13	Materials Inventory	10,300.00						10,300.00	
14	Estimated Returns Inventory	65.00		(c)	585.00			650.00	
15	Office Supplies	6,200.00				(g)	5,245.00	955.00	
16	Factory Supplies	5,730.00				(h)	4,950.00	780.00	
17	Prepaid Insurance	7,300.00				(i)	6,200.00	1,100.00	
18	Land	75,000.00						75,000.00	
19	Factory Building	115,000.00						115,000.00	
20	Accum. Depr.—Factory Building		23,000.00			(j)	6,000.00		29,000.00
21	Factory Equipment	60,000.00						60,000.00	
22	Accum. Depr.—Factory Equip.		12,000.00			(k)	7,500.00		19,500.00
23	Accounts Payable		18,300.00						18,300.00
24	Customer Refunds Payable		115.00			(b)	1,005.00		1,120.00
25	Income Tax Payable					(m)	3,800.00		3,800.00
26	Interest Payable					(e)	1,350.00		1,350.00
27	Bonds Payable		80,000.00						80,000.00
28	Capital Stock		70,000.00						70,000.00
29	Paid-In Capital in Excess of Par		25,000.00						25,000.00
30	Retained Earnings		99,190.00						99,190.00
31	Cash Dividends	10,000.00						10,000.00	
32	Sales		360,200.00						360,200.00
33	Sales Returns and Allowances	5,700.00		(b)	1,005.00			6,705.00	
34	Interest Revenue		600.00			(d)	165.00		765.00
35	Factory Overhead	83,200.00	98,600.00	(h)	4,950.00	(a)	2,850.00	107,850.00	107,850.00
36				(i)	6,200.00	(l)	6,400.00		
37				(j)	6,000.00				
38				(k)	7,500.00				
39	Cost of Goods Sold	198,900.00		(l)	6,400.00	(c)	585.00	204,715.00	
40	Salaries Expense	90,000.00						90,000.00	
41	Office Supplies Expense			(g)	5,245.00			5,245.00	
42	Bad Debt Expense			(f)	2,475.00			2,475.00	
43	Utilities Expense—Office	5,930.00						5,930.00	
44	Interest Expense	7,400.00		(e)	1,350.00			8,750.00	
45	Income Tax Expense	3,000.00		(m)	3,800.00			6,800.00	
46		787,925.00	787,925.00		48,525.00		48,525.00	819,470.00	819,470.00
47								438,470.00	468,815.00
48	Net Income							30,345.00	

Problem 7 (Continued)

Data for adjusting the accounts:

(a)	Factory overhead (to be applied to work in process ending inventory)	$2,850
(b)	Estimate of this year's sales that will be returned next year	1,120
(c)	Cost of goods expected to be returned	650
	Interest accruals:	
(d)	Interest receivable	165
(e)	Interest payable	1,350
(f)	Estimate of uncollectible accounts, based on an aging of accounts receivable	3,395
(g)	Office supplies consumed	5,245
(h)	Factory supplies consumed	4,950
(i)	Insurance on factory building and equipment expired	6,200
	Depreciation:	
(j)	Factory building	6,000
(k)	Factory equipment	7,500
(l)	Underapplied factory overhead	6,400
(m)	Provision for corporate income taxes	3,800

Required:

1. Journalize the adjusting entries in the general journal below and on page 491.
2. Journalize the closing entries in the general journal on page 492.
3. Journalize the reversing entries as of January 2, 20-5, in the general journal on page 493.

1.

GENERAL JOURNAL

PAGE

	DATE		DESCRIPTION	POST. REF.	DEBIT	CREDIT	
1							1
2							2
3							3
4							4
5							5
6							6
7							7
8							8
9							9
10							10
11							11
12							12
13							13
14							14
15							15
16							16

Problem 7 (Continued)

1.

GENERAL JOURNAL

PAGE

	DATE	DESCRIPTION	POST. REF.	DEBIT	CREDIT	
1						1
2						2
3						3
4						4
5						5
6						6
7						7
8						8
9						9
10						10
11						11
12						12
13						13
14						14
15						15
16						16
17						17
18						18
19						19
20						20
21						21
22						22
23						23
24						24
25						25
26						26
27						27
28						28
29						29
30						30
31						31
32						32
33						33

Problem 7 (Continued)

2.

GENERAL JOURNAL

PAGE

DATE		DESCRIPTION	POST. REF.	DEBIT	CREDIT

Problem 7 (Concluded)

3.

GENERAL JOURNAL

PAGE

	DATE		DESCRIPTION	POST. REF.	DEBIT	CREDIT	
1							1
2							2
3							3
4							4
5							5
6							6
7							7
8							8
9							9
10							10
11							11
12							12
13							13
14							14
15							15
16							16
17							17
18							18
19							19
20							20
21							21
22							22
23							23
24							24
25							25
26							26
27							27
28							28
29							29
30							30
31							31
32							32
33							33

Working Papers

Chapters 16-27

Exercise 16-1A

Exercise 16-2A

1.

GENERAL JOURNAL PAGE

	DATE		DESCRIPTION	POST. REF.	DEBIT	CREDIT	
1							1
2							2
3							3
4							4
5							5

2.

GENERAL JOURNAL PAGE

	DATE		DESCRIPTION	POST. REF.	DEBIT	CREDIT	
1							1
2							2
3							3
4							4
5							5

Exercise 16-3A

1.

GENERAL JOURNAL PAGE

	DATE		DESCRIPTION	POST. REF.	DEBIT	CREDIT	
1							1
2							2
3							3
4							4
5							5

2.

GENERAL JOURNAL PAGE

	DATE		DESCRIPTION	POST. REF.	DEBIT	CREDIT	
1							1
2							2
3							3
4							4
5							5

Exercise 16-4A

GENERAL JOURNAL PAGE

	DATE		DESCRIPTION	POST. REF.	DEBIT	CREDIT	
1							1
2							2
3							3
4							4
5							5
6							6
7							7
8							8
9							9
10							10
11							11
12							12
13							13
14							14
15							15
16							16

Exercise 16-5A

1. a.

GENERAL JOURNAL PAGE

	DATE		DESCRIPTION	POST. REF.	DEBIT	CREDIT	
1							1
2							2
3							3
4							4

b.

GENERAL JOURNAL PAGE

	DATE		DESCRIPTION	POST. REF.	DEBIT	CREDIT	
1							1
2							2
3							3
4							4

Exercise 16-5A (Concluded)

2. a.

GENERAL JOURNAL PAGE

	DATE		DESCRIPTION	POST. REF.	DEBIT	CREDIT	
1							1
2							2
3							3
4							4
5							5

b.

GENERAL JOURNAL PAGE

	DATE		DESCRIPTION	POST. REF.	DEBIT	CREDIT	
1							1
2							2
3							3
4							4
5							5

Exercise 16-6A

GENERAL JOURNAL PAGE

	DATE		DESCRIPTION	POST. REF.	DEBIT	CREDIT	
1							1
2							2
3							3
4							4
5							5
6							6
7							7
8							8
9							9
10							10
11							11
12							12
13							13

Name ____________________

Exercise 16-7A

GENERAL JOURNAL

PAGE

DATE		DESCRIPTION	POST. REF.	DEBIT	CREDIT

Problem 16-8A

1. and 2. **GENERAL JOURNAL** PAGE 6

DATE		DESCRIPTION	POST. REF.	DEBIT	CREDIT

Problem 16-8A (Concluded)

GENERAL JOURNAL

PAGE 7

	DATE		DESCRIPTION	POST. REF.	DEBIT	CREDIT	
1							1
2							2
3							3
4							4

GENERAL LEDGER

ACCOUNT Allowance for Doubtful Accounts ACCOUNT NO. 122.1

DATE		ITEM	POST. REF.	DEBIT	CREDIT	BALANCE DEBIT	BALANCE CREDIT
20-- Jan.	1	Balance	✓				43 0 0 0 00

ACCOUNT Income Summary ACCOUNT NO. 313

DATE		ITEM	POST. REF.	DEBIT	CREDIT	BALANCE DEBIT	BALANCE CREDIT

ACCOUNT Bad Debt Expense ACCOUNT NO. 532

DATE		ITEM	POST. REF.	DEBIT	CREDIT	BALANCE DEBIT	BALANCE CREDIT

3.

Problem 16-9A

1. a.

GENERAL JOURNAL

PAGE

	DATE		DESCRIPTION	POST. REF.	DEBIT	CREDIT	
1							1
2							2
3							3
4							4

b.

GENERAL JOURNAL

PAGE

	DATE		DESCRIPTION	POST. REF.	DEBIT	CREDIT	
1							1
2							2
3							3
4							4

2. a.

GENERAL JOURNAL

PAGE

	DATE		DESCRIPTION	POST. REF.	DEBIT	CREDIT	
1							1
2							2
3							3
4							4

Problem 16-9A (Concluded)

b.

GENERAL JOURNAL

PAGE

DATE		DESCRIPTION	POST. REF.	DEBIT	CREDIT	
1						1
2						2
3						3
4						4

Problem 16-10A

1.

	A	B	C	D
1	Age Interval	Balance	Estimated Percent Uncollectible	Estimated Amount Uncollectible
2				
3				
4				
5				
6				
7				
8				
9				
10				

2.

GENERAL JOURNAL

PAGE

DATE		DESCRIPTION	POST. REF.	DEBIT	CREDIT	
1						1
2						2
3						3
4						4

Problem 16-11A

GENERAL JOURNAL

PAGE

DATE		DESCRIPTION	POST. REF.	DEBIT	CREDIT

Exercise 16-1B

Exercise 16-2B

1.

GENERAL JOURNAL

PAGE

	DATE	DESCRIPTION	POST. REF.	DEBIT	CREDIT	
1						1
2						2
3						3
4						4
5						5

2.

GENERAL JOURNAL

PAGE

	DATE	DESCRIPTION	POST. REF.	DEBIT	CREDIT	
1						1
2						2
3						3
4						4
5						5

Exercise 16-3B

1.

GENERAL JOURNAL

PAGE

	DATE	DESCRIPTION	POST. REF.	DEBIT	CREDIT	
1						1
2						2
3						3
4						4
5						5

2.

GENERAL JOURNAL

PAGE

	DATE	DESCRIPTION	POST. REF.	DEBIT	CREDIT	
1						1
2						2
3						3
4						4
5						5

Exercise 16-4B

GENERAL JOURNAL PAGE

	DATE		DESCRIPTION	POST. REF.	DEBIT	CREDIT	
1							1
2							2
3							3
4							4
5							5
6							6
7							7
8							8
9							9
10							10
11							11
12							12
13							13
14							14
15							15
16							16

Exercise 16-5B

1. a.

GENERAL JOURNAL PAGE

	DATE		DESCRIPTION	POST. REF.	DEBIT	CREDIT	
1							1
2							2
3							3
4							4

b.

GENERAL JOURNAL PAGE

	DATE		DESCRIPTION	POST. REF.	DEBIT	CREDIT	
1							1
2							2
3							3
4							4

Exercise 16-5B (Concluded)

2. a.

GENERAL JOURNAL PAGE

	DATE		DESCRIPTION	POST. REF.	DEBIT	CREDIT	
1							1
2							2
3							3
4							4
5							5

b.

GENERAL JOURNAL PAGE

	DATE		DESCRIPTION	POST. REF.	DEBIT	CREDIT	
1							1
2							2
3							3
4							4
5							5

Exercise 16-6B

GENERAL JOURNAL PAGE

	DATE		DESCRIPTION	POST. REF.	DEBIT	CREDIT	
1							1
2							2
3							3
4							4
5							5
6							6
7							7
8							8
9							9
10							10
11							11
12							12
13							13

Exercise 16-7B

GENERAL JOURNAL

PAGE

DATE		DESCRIPTION	POST. REF.	DEBIT	CREDIT

Problem 16-8B

1. and 2.

GENERAL JOURNAL

PAGE 6

	DATE		DESCRIPTION	POST. REF.	DEBIT	CREDIT	
1							1
2							2
3							3
4							4
5							5
6							6
7							7
8							8
9							9
10							10
11							11
12							12
13							13
14							14
15							15
16							16
17							17
18							18
19							19
20							20
21							21
22							22
23							23
24							24
25							25
26							26
27							27
28							28
29							29
30							30
31							31
32							32
33							33
34							34
35							35
36							36
37							37
38							38
39							39

Problem 16-8B (Concluded)

GENERAL JOURNAL

PAGE 7

	DATE	DESCRIPTION	POST. REF.	DEBIT	CREDIT	
1						1
2						2
3						3
4						4

GENERAL LEDGER

ACCOUNT Allowance for Doubtful Accounts ACCOUNT NO. 122.1

DATE	ITEM	POST. REF.	DEBIT	CREDIT	BALANCE DEBIT	BALANCE CREDIT
20-- Jan. 1	Balance	✓				49 8 5 0 00

ACCOUNT Income Summary ACCOUNT NO. 313

DATE	ITEM	POST. REF.	DEBIT	CREDIT	BALANCE DEBIT	BALANCE CREDIT

ACCOUNT Bad Debt Expense ACCOUNT NO. 532

DATE	ITEM	POST. REF.	DEBIT	CREDIT	BALANCE DEBIT	BALANCE CREDIT

3.

Problem 16-9B

1. a. **GENERAL JOURNAL** PAGE

	DATE		DESCRIPTION	POST. REF.	DEBIT	CREDIT	
1							1
2							2
3							3
4							4

b. **GENERAL JOURNAL** PAGE

	DATE		DESCRIPTION	POST. REF.	DEBIT	CREDIT	
1							1
2							2
3							3
4							4

2. a. **GENERAL JOURNAL** PAGE

	DATE		DESCRIPTION	POST. REF.	DEBIT	CREDIT	
1							1
2							2
3							3
4							4

Problem 16-9B (Concluded)

b.

GENERAL JOURNAL

PAGE

	DATE		DESCRIPTION	POST. REF.	DEBIT	CREDIT	
1							1
2							2
3							3
4							4

Problem 16-10B

1.

	A	B	C	D
1	**Age Interval**	**Balance**	**Estimated Percent Uncollectible**	**Estimated Amount Uncollectible**
2				
3				
4				
5				
6				
7				
8				
9				
10				

2.

GENERAL JOURNAL

PAGE

	DATE		DESCRIPTION	POST. REF.	DEBIT	CREDIT	
1							1
2							2
3							3
4							4

Problem 16-11B

GENERAL JOURNAL

PAGE

DATE		DESCRIPTION	POST. REF.	DEBIT	CREDIT

Mastery Problem

1., 3., and 4.

GENERAL LEDGER—SAM

ACCOUNT Cash ACCOUNT NO. 101

DATE		ITEM	POST. REF.	DEBIT	CREDIT	BALANCE	
						DEBIT	CREDIT

ACCOUNT Accounts Receivable ACCOUNT NO. 122

DATE		ITEM	POST. REF.	DEBIT	CREDIT	BALANCE	
						DEBIT	CREDIT

ACCOUNT Allowance for Doubtful Accounts ACCOUNT NO. 122.1

DATE		ITEM	POST. REF.	DEBIT	CREDIT	BALANCE	
						DEBIT	CREDIT

ACCOUNT Sales ACCOUNT NO. 401

DATE		ITEM	POST. REF.	DEBIT	CREDIT	BALANCE	
						DEBIT	CREDIT

Mastery Problem (Continued)

4.

ACCOUNT Bad Debt Expense ACCOUNT NO. 532

DATE		ITEM	POST. REF.	DEBIT	CREDIT	BALANCE	
						DEBIT	CREDIT

5.

Mastery Problem (Continued)

2. and 4.

GENERAL JOURNAL

PAGE 4

DATE		DESCRIPTION	POST. REF.	DEBIT	CREDIT

Mastery Problem (Continued)

6. and 8.

GENERAL JOURNAL

PAGE 4

	DATE		DESCRIPTION	POST. REF.	DEBIT	CREDIT	
1							1
2							2
3							3
4							4
5							5
6							6
7							7
8							8
9							9
10							10
11							11
12							12
13							13
14							14
15							15
16							16
17							17
18							18
19							19
20							20
21							21
22							22
23							23
24							24
25							25
26							26
27							27
28							28
29							29
30							30
31							31
32							32
33							33
34							34
35							35

Mastery Problem (Continued)

1., 7., and 8.

GENERAL LEDGER—ROBERT

ACCOUNT Cash ACCOUNT NO. 101

DATE	ITEM	POST. REF.	DEBIT	CREDIT	BALANCE	
					DEBIT	CREDIT

ACCOUNT Accounts Receivable ACCOUNT NO. 122

DATE	ITEM	POST. REF.	DEBIT	CREDIT	BALANCE	
					DEBIT	CREDIT

ACCOUNT Allowance for Doubtful Accounts ACCOUNT NO. 122.1

DATE	ITEM	POST. REF.	DEBIT	CREDIT	BALANCE	
					DEBIT	CREDIT

ACCOUNT Sales ACCOUNT NO. 401

DATE	ITEM	POST. REF.	DEBIT	CREDIT	BALANCE	
					DEBIT	CREDIT

Mastery Problem (Concluded)

8.

ACCOUNT Bad Debt Expense ACCOUNT NO. 532

DATE		ITEM	POST. REF.	DEBIT	CREDIT	BALANCE DEBIT	BALANCE CREDIT

AGING SCHEDULE OF ACCOUNTS RECEIVABLE FOR ROBERT

	A	B	C	D	E	F	G	H
1				Number of Days Past Due				
2	Customer	Total	Not Yet Due	1–30	31–60	61–90	91–120	Over 120
3								
4								
5								
6								
7								
8								
9								
10								
11								
12								
13								
14								

9.

Challenge Problem

1.

GENERAL JOURNAL

PAGE

	DATE		DESCRIPTION	POST. REF.	DEBIT	CREDIT	
1							1
2							2
3							3
4							4
5							5
6							6

2.

GENERAL JOURNAL

PAGE

	DATE		DESCRIPTION	POST. REF.	DEBIT	CREDIT	
1							1
2							2
3							3
4							4
5							5
6							6
7							7

Challenge Problem (Concluded)

3. a.

b.

GENERAL JOURNAL

PAGE

	DATE		DESCRIPTION	POST. REF.	DEBIT	CREDIT	
1							1
2							2
3							3
4							4
5							5
6							6
7							7

Name ______________________________

Exercise 17-1A

Date of Note	Due Date	Time in Days
May 4	July 17	______
August 17	October 1	______
July 5	September 5	______
December 11	February 5	______
March 24	May 16	______
January 6	March 18	______

Exercise 17-2A

Principal	Rate	Time	Interest
$5,000	6.00%	30 days	______
1,000	7.50	60	______
4,500	8.00	120	______
950	6.80	95	______
1,250	7.25	102	______
2,900	7.00	90	______

Exercise 17-3A

Date of Note	Term of Note	Due Date
August 12	90 days	______
September 1	60	______
January 3	120	______
March 18	88	______
June 11	200	______
May 17	38	______

Exercise 17-4A

GENERAL JOURNAL

PAGE

	DATE		DESCRIPTION	POST. REF.	DEBIT	CREDIT	
1							1
2							2
3							3
4							4
5							5
6							6
7							7
8							8
9							9
10							10
11							11
12							12
13							13
14							14
15							15
16							16
17							17
18							18
19							19
20							20
21							21
22							22
23							23
24							24
25							25
26							26
27							27
28							28
29							29
30							30
31							31
32							32
33							33
34							34
35							35

Exercise 17-5A

GENERAL JOURNAL

PAGE

	DATE		DESCRIPTION	POST. REF.	DEBIT	CREDIT	
1							1
2							2
3							3
4							4
5							5
6							6
7							7
8							8
9							9
10							10
11							11
12							12
13							13
14							14
15							15
16							16
17							17
18							18
19							19
20							20
21							21
22							22
23							23
24							24
25							25
26							26
27							27
28							28
29							29
30							30
31							31
32							32
33							33
34							34
35							35
36							36

Exercise 17-6A

GENERAL JOURNAL

PAGE

	DATE		DESCRIPTION	POST. REF.	DEBIT	CREDIT	
1							1
2							2
3							3
4							4
5							5
6							6
7							7
8							8
9							9

Exercise 17-7A

GENERAL JOURNAL

PAGE

	DATE		DESCRIPTION	POST. REF.	DEBIT	CREDIT	
1							1
2							2
3							3
4							4
5							5
6							6
7							7
8							8
9							9
10							10
11							11
12							12
13							13
14							14
15							15
16							16
17							17
18							18
19							19
20							20

Exercise 17-8A

GENERAL JOURNAL

PAGE

DATE		DESCRIPTION	POST. REF.	DEBIT	CREDIT

Exercise 17-9A

GENERAL JOURNAL

PAGE

DATE		DESCRIPTION	POST. REF.	DEBIT	CREDIT

Problem 17-10A

GENERAL JOURNAL

PAGE

DATE		DESCRIPTION	POST. REF.	DEBIT	CREDIT

Problem 17-10A (Concluded)

GENERAL JOURNAL

PAGE

	DATE		DESCRIPTION	POST. REF.	DEBIT	CREDIT	
1							1
2							2
3							3
4							4
5							5
6							6
7							7
8							8
9							9
10							10
11							11
12							12
13							13
14							14
15							15
16							16
17							17
18							18
19							19
20							20
21							21
22							22
23							23
24							24
25							25
26							26
27							27
28							28
29							29
30							30
31							31
32							32
33							33
34							34
35							35
36							36

Problem 17-11A

GENERAL JOURNAL

PAGE

DATE		DESCRIPTION	POST. REF.	DEBIT	CREDIT

Problem 17-11A (Concluded)

GENERAL JOURNAL

PAGE

DATE		DESCRIPTION	POST. REF.	DEBIT	CREDIT

Problem 17-12A

1.

2.

GENERAL JOURNAL

PAGE

	DATE		DESCRIPTION	POST. REF.	DEBIT	CREDIT	
1							1
2							2
3							3
4							4

Problem 17-13A

GENERAL JOURNAL

PAGE

	DATE		DESCRIPTION	POST. REF.	DEBIT	CREDIT	
1							1
2							2
3							3
4							4
5							5
6							6
7							7
8							8
9							9
10							10
11							11
12							12
13							13
14							14
15							15
16							16
17							17
18							18

Problem 17-13A (Concluded)

GENERAL JOURNAL

PAGE

DATE		DESCRIPTION	POST. REF.	DEBIT	CREDIT

Problem 17-14A

1.

2.

GENERAL JOURNAL

PAGE

	DATE		DESCRIPTION	POST. REF.	DEBIT	CREDIT	
1							1
2							2
3							3
4							4
5							5
6							6
7							7
8							8
9							9
10							10
11							11
12							12
13							13
14							14
15							15
16							16
17							17
18							18
19							19

Exercise 17-1B

Date of Note	Due Date	Time in Days
August 17	October 10	
January 12	March 10	
July 15	September 13	
December 3	February 1	
April 11	July 6	
October 6	December 18	

Exercise 17-2B

Principal	Rate	Time	Interest
$4,000	7.00%	60 days	
3,000	6.50	30	
7,500	8.00	150	
850	7.90	99	
2,250	7.55	122	
1,900	6.80	82	

Exercise 17-3B

Date of Note	Term of Note	Due Date
July 11	45 days	
December 23	90	
April 18	120	
October 3	77	
January 1	180	
August 13	65	

Exercise 17-4B

GENERAL JOURNAL

PAGE

	DATE	DESCRIPTION	POST. REF.	DEBIT	CREDIT	
1						1
2						2
3						3
4						4
5						5
6						6
7						7
8						8
9						9
10						10
11						11
12						12
13						13
14						14
15						15
16						16
17						17
18						18
19						19
20						20
21						21
22						22
23						23
24						24
25						25
26						26
27						27
28						28
29						29
30						30
31						31
32						32
33						33
34						34
35						35
36						36

Exercise 17-5B

GENERAL JOURNAL

PAGE

DATE		DESCRIPTION	POST. REF.	DEBIT	CREDIT

Exercise 17-6B

GENERAL JOURNAL PAGE

	DATE		DESCRIPTION	POST. REF.	DEBIT	CREDIT	
1							1
2							2
3							3
4							4
5							5
6							6
7							7
8							8
9							9
10							10

Exercise 17-7B

GENERAL JOURNAL PAGE

	DATE		DESCRIPTION	POST. REF.	DEBIT	CREDIT	
1							1
2							2
3							3
4							4
5							5
6							6
7							7
8							8
9							9
10							10
11							11
12							12
13							13
14							14
15							15
16							16
17							17
18							18
19							19
20							20

Exercise 17-8B

GENERAL JOURNAL PAGE

	DATE		DESCRIPTION	POST. REF.	DEBIT	CREDIT	
1							1
2							2
3							3
4							4
5							5
6							6
7							7
8							8
9							9
10							10
11							11
12							12
13							13
14							14
15							15
16							16
17							17
18							18
19							19
20							20

Exercise 17-9B

GENERAL JOURNAL PAGE

	DATE		DESCRIPTION	POST. REF.	DEBIT	CREDIT	
1							1
2							2
3							3
4							4
5							5
6							6
7							7
8							8
9							9
10							10

Problem 17-10B

GENERAL JOURNAL

PAGE

DATE		DESCRIPTION	POST. REF.	DEBIT	CREDIT

Problem 17-10B (Concluded)

GENERAL JOURNAL

PAGE

DATE		DESCRIPTION	POST. REF.	DEBIT	CREDIT

Problem 17-11B

GENERAL JOURNAL

PAGE

	DATE		DESCRIPTION	POST. REF.	DEBIT	CREDIT	
1							1
2							2
3							3
4							4
5							5
6							6
7							7
8							8
9							9
10							10
11							11
12							12
13							13
14							14
15							15
16							16
17							17
18							18
19							19
20							20
21							21
22							22
23							23
24							24
25							25
26							26
27							27
28							28
29							29
30							30
31							31
32							32
33							33
34							34
35							35
36							36

Problem 17-11B (Concluded)

GENERAL JOURNAL

PAGE

DATE		DESCRIPTION	POST. REF.	DEBIT	CREDIT

Problem 17-12B

1.

2.

GENERAL JOURNAL

PAGE

	DATE		DESCRIPTION	POST. REF.	DEBIT	CREDIT	
1							1
2							2
3							3
4							4

Problem 17-13B

GENERAL JOURNAL

PAGE

	DATE		DESCRIPTION	POST. REF.	DEBIT	CREDIT	
1							1
2							2
3							3
4							4
5							5
6							6
7							7
8							8
9							9
10							10
11							11
12							12
13							13
14							14
15							15
16							16
17							17
18							18

Problem 17-13B (Concluded)

GENERAL JOURNAL

PAGE

	DATE		DESCRIPTION	POST. REF.	DEBIT	CREDIT	
1							1
2							2
3							3
4							4
5							5
6							6
7							7
8							8
9							9
10							10
11							11
12							12
13							13
14							14
15							15
16							16
17							17
18							18
19							19
20							20
21							21
22							22
23							23
24							24
25							25
26							26
27							27
28							28
29							29
30							30
31							31
32							32
33							33
34							34
35							35
36							36

Problem 17-14B

1.

2.

GENERAL JOURNAL PAGE

	DATE		DESCRIPTION	POST. REF.	DEBIT	CREDIT	
1							1
2							2
3							3
4							4
5							5
6							6
7							7
8							8
9							9
10							10
11							11
12							12
13							13
14							14
15							15
16							16
17							17
18							18
19							19

Mastery Problem

1. and 2.

GENERAL JOURNAL

PAGE

	DATE	DESCRIPTION	POST. REF.	DEBIT	CREDIT	
1						1
2						2
3						3
4						4
5						5
6						6
7						7
8						8
9						9
10						10
11						11
12						12
13						13
14						14
15						15
16						16
17						17
18						18
19						19
20						20
21						21
22						22
23						23
24						24
25						25
26						26
27						27
28						28
29						29
30						30
31						31
32						32
33						33
34						34
35						35

Mastery Problem (Concluded)

GENERAL JOURNAL

PAGE

	DATE		DESCRIPTION	POST. REF.	DEBIT	CREDIT	
1							1
2							2
3							3
4							4
5							5
6							6
7							7
8							8
9							9
10							10
11							11
12							12
13							13
14							14
15							15
16							16
17							17
18							18
19							19
20							20
21							21
22							22
23							23
24							24
25							25
26							26
27							27
28							28
29							29
30							30
31							31
32							32
33							33
34							34
35							35
36							36

Challenge Problem

Mirror Co.

GENERAL JOURNAL

PAGE

DATE		DESCRIPTION	POST. REF.	DEBIT	CREDIT

Challenge Problem (Concluded)

Other Party (Rosman Co., Kaw County Bank, or Lawrence Bank)

GENERAL JOURNAL

PAGE

	DATE	DESCRIPTION	POST. REF.	DEBIT	CREDIT	
1						1
2						2
3						3
4						4
5						5
6						6
7						7
8						8
9						9
10						10
11						11
12						12
13						13
14						14
15						15
16						16
17						17
18						18
19						19
20						20
21						21
22						22
23						23
24						24
25						25
26						26
27						27
28						28
29						29
30						30
31						31
32						32
33						33
34						34
35						35

Exercise 18-1A

	Yes	No
Debit Land?		
Real estate fees	________	________
Cost to remove old buildings	________	________
Cost to pave parking areas	________	________
Tax assessment for streets	________	________
Debit Building?		
Cost of land on which the building is located	________	________
Legal fees related to purchase	________	________
Taxes related to purchase	________	________
Realtor fees	________	________
Interest on construction loan while building was under construction	________	________
Debit Equipment?		
Transportation charges	________	________
Insurance while in transit	________	________
Installation costs	________	________
Interest on loan to buy equipment	________	________

Exercise 18-2A

Exercise 18-2A (Concluded)

Exercise 18-3A

Exercise 18-4A

GENERAL JOURNAL

PAGE

	DATE		DESCRIPTION	POST. REF.	DEBIT	CREDIT	
1							1
2							2
3							3
4							4
5							5
6							6
7							7
8							8
9							9
10							10
11							11
12							12
13							13
14							14
15							15
16							16
17							17
18							18
19							19

Exercise 18-5A

1.

GENERAL JOURNAL

PAGE

	DATE		DESCRIPTION	POST. REF.	DEBIT	CREDIT	
1							1
2							2
3							3
4							4
5							5
6							6
7							7
8							8
9							9
10							10
11							11
12							12
13							13
14							14
15							15

2.

GENERAL JOURNAL

PAGE

	DATE		DESCRIPTION	POST. REF.	DEBIT	CREDIT	
1							1
2							2
3							3
4							4
5							5
6							6
7							7
8							8
9							9
10							10
11							11
12							12
13							13
14							14
15							15

Exercise 18-6A

1.

GENERAL JOURNAL

PAGE

	DATE		DESCRIPTION	POST. REF.	DEBIT	CREDIT	
1							1
2							2
3							3
4							4
5							5
6							6
7							7
8							8
9							9
10							10
11							11
12							12
13							13
14							14
15							15

2.

GENERAL JOURNAL

PAGE

	DATE		DESCRIPTION	POST. REF.	DEBIT	CREDIT	
1							1
2							2
3							3
4							4
5							5
6							6
7							7
8							8
9							9
10							10
11							11
12							12
13							13
14							14
15							15

Problem 18-7A

1. a.

Year	Annual Depreciation	Ending Book Value

1. b.

Year	Beginning Book Value	Rate	Annual Depreciation	Ending Book Value

1. c.

Year	Depreciable Cost	Rate	Annual Depreciation	Ending Book Value

Problem 18-7A (Concluded)

2.

Year	Original Cost	MACRS Depreciation Rates 7-Year Class of Property	Depreciation Expense

Problem 18-8A

Year	Beginning Book Value	Annual Depreciation	Ending Book Value

Problem 18-9A

1.

2.

GENERAL JOURNAL PAGE

	DATE		DESCRIPTION	POST. REF.	DEBIT	CREDIT	
1							1
2							2
3							3
4							4
5							5
6							6
7							7
8							8

Problem 18-10A

1.

GENERAL JOURNAL PAGE

	DATE	DESCRIPTION	POST. REF.	DEBIT	CREDIT	
1						1
2						2
3						3
4						4
5						5
6						6
7						7
8						8
9						9

2.

GENERAL JOURNAL PAGE

	DATE	DESCRIPTION	POST. REF.	DEBIT	CREDIT	
1						1
2						2
3						3
4						4
5						5
6						6
7						7

3.

Problem 18-11A

GENERAL JOURNAL

PAGE

DATE		DESCRIPTION	POST. REF.	DEBIT	CREDIT

Problem 18-12A

1.

2.

GENERAL JOURNAL PAGE

	DATE		DESCRIPTION	POST. REF.	DEBIT	CREDIT	
1							1
2							2
3							3
4							4
5							5
6							6

Problem 18-13A

1.

2.

GENERAL JOURNAL PAGE

	DATE		DESCRIPTION	POST. REF.	DEBIT	CREDIT	
1							1
2							2
3							3
4							4
5							5
6							6
7							7
8							8

Exercise 18-1B

Exercise 18-2B

Exercise 18-2B (Concluded)

Exercise 18-3B

Exercise 18-4B

GENERAL JOURNAL PAGE

	DATE		DESCRIPTION	POST. REF.	DEBIT	CREDIT	
1							1
2							2
3							3
4							4
5							5
6							6
7							7
8							8
9							9
10							10
11							11
12							12
13							13
14							14
15							15
16							16
17							17
18							18
19							19
20							20

Exercise 18-5B

1.

GENERAL JOURNAL

PAGE

	DATE		DESCRIPTION	POST. REF.	DEBIT	CREDIT	
1							1
2							2
3							3
4							4
5							5
6							6
7							7
8							8
9							9
10							10
11							11
12							12
13							13
14							14
15							15

2.

GENERAL JOURNAL

PAGE

	DATE		DESCRIPTION	POST. REF.	DEBIT	CREDIT	
1							1
2							2
3							3
4							4
5							5
6							6
7							7
8							8
9							9
10							10
11							11
12							12
13							13
14							14
15							15

Exercise 18-6B

1.

GENERAL JOURNAL

PAGE

	DATE		DESCRIPTION	POST. REF.	DEBIT	CREDIT	
1							1
2							2
3							3
4							4
5							5
6							6
7							7
8							8
9							9
10							10
11							11
12							12
13							13
14							14
15							15

2.

GENERAL JOURNAL

PAGE

	DATE		DESCRIPTION	POST. REF.	DEBIT	CREDIT	
1							1
2							2
3							3
4							4
5							5
6							6
7							7
8							8
9							9
10							10
11							11
12							12
13							13
14							14
15							15

Problem 18-7B

1. a.

Year	Annual Depreciation	Ending Book Value

1. b.

Year	Beginning Book Value	Rate	Annual Depreciation	Ending Book Value

1. c.

Year	Depreciable Cost	Rate	Annual Depreciation	Ending Book Value

Problem 18-7B (Concluded)

1.

Year	Original Cost	MACRS Depreciation Rates 7-Year Class of Property	Depreciation Expense

Problem 18-8B

Year	Beginning Book Value	Annual Depreciation	Ending Book Value

Problem 18-9B

1.

2.

GENERAL JOURNAL PAGE

	DATE		DESCRIPTION	POST. REF.	DEBIT	CREDIT	
1							1
2							2
3							3
4							4
5							5
6							6
7							7
8							8
9							9

Problem 18-10B

1.

GENERAL JOURNAL PAGE

	DATE		DESCRIPTION	POST. REF.	DEBIT	CREDIT	
1							1
2							2
3							3
4							4
5							5
6							6
7							7

2.

GENERAL JOURNAL PAGE

	DATE		DESCRIPTION	POST. REF.	DEBIT	CREDIT	
1							1
2							2
3							3
4							4
5							5
6							6
7							7

3.

Name ______________________________

Problem 18-11B

GENERAL JOURNAL

PAGE

	DATE		DESCRIPTION	POST. REF.	DEBIT	CREDIT	
1							1
2							2
3							3
4							4
5							5
6							6
7							7
8							8
9							9
10							10
11							11
12							12
13							13
14							14
15							15
16							16
17							17
18							18
19							19
20							20
21							21
22							22
23							23
24							24
25							25
26							26
27							27
28							28
29							29
30							30
31							31
32							32
33							33
34							34
35							35
36							36

Problem 18-12B

1.

2.

GENERAL JOURNAL PAGE

	DATE		DESCRIPTION	POST. REF.	DEBIT	CREDIT	
1							1
2							2
3							3
4							4
5							5
6							6

Problem 18-13B

1.

2.

GENERAL JOURNAL PAGE

	DATE		DESCRIPTION	POST. REF.	DEBIT	CREDIT	
1							1
2							2
3							3
4							4
5							5
6							6
7							7
8							8
9							9
10							10

Mastery Problem

1.

GENERAL JOURNAL

PAGE

DATE		DESCRIPTION	POST. REF.	DEBIT	CREDIT

Mastery Problem (Concluded)

2.

GENERAL JOURNAL

PAGE

	DATE	DESCRIPTION	POST. REF.	DEBIT	CREDIT	
1						1
2						2
3						3
4						4
5						5
6						6
7						7
8						8
9						9
10						10
11						11
12						12
13						13
14						14
15						15
16						16
17						17
18						18
19						19
20						20
21						21
22						22
23						23
24						24
25						25
26						26
27						27
28						28
29						29
30						30
31						31
32						32
33						33
34						34

Challenge Problem

1. Computer Equipment	Straight-Line Depreciation Year							
	20-1	20-2	20-3	20-4	20-5	20-6	20-7	20-8

2. Computer Equipment	MACRS Depreciation Year							
	20-1	20-2	20-3	20-4	20-5	20-6	20-7	20-8

3. ____________________

4. ____________________

____

____

5.

____

____

Name ______________________________

Exercise 19-1A

GENERAL JOURNAL PAGE

	DATE		DESCRIPTION	POST. REF.	DEBIT	CREDIT	
1							1
2							2
3							3
4							4
5							5
6							6
7							7
8							8
9							9
10							10

Exercise 19-2A

Exercise 19-3A

1.

2.

Exercise 19-4A

1.

GENERAL JOURNAL PAGE

	DATE		DESCRIPTION	POST. REF.	DEBIT	CREDIT	
1							1
2							2
3							3
4							4
5							5
6							6
7							7
8							8
9							9
10							10

2.

Exercise 19-5A

GENERAL JOURNAL PAGE

	DATE		DESCRIPTION	POST. REF.	DEBIT	CREDIT	
1							1
2							2
3							3
4							4
5							5
6							6
7							7
8							8
9							9
10							10

Problem 19-6A

GENERAL JOURNAL

PAGE

DATE		DESCRIPTION	POST. REF.	DEBIT	CREDIT
1					
2					
3					
4					
5					
6					
7					
8					
9					
10					
11					
12					
13					
14					
15					
16					
17					
18					
19					
20					
21					
22					
23					
24					
25					
26					
27					
28					
29					
30					
31					
32					
33					
34					
35					

Problem 19-7A

1.

2.

Problem 19-7A (Concluded)

3.

GENERAL JOURNAL

PAGE

	DATE		DESCRIPTION	POST. REF.	DEBIT	CREDIT	
1							1
2							2
3							3
4							4
5							5
6							6
7							7
8							8
9							9
10							10
11							11
12							12
13							13
14							14
15							15
16							16
17							17
18							18

Problem 19-8A

1.

GENERAL JOURNAL

PAGE

	DATE		DESCRIPTION	POST. REF.	DEBIT	CREDIT	
1							1
2							2
3							3
4							4
5							5
6							6
7							7
8							8
9							9
10							10

Problem 19-8A (Concluded)

2.

GENERAL JOURNAL

PAGE

	DATE		DESCRIPTION	POST. REF.	DEBIT	CREDIT	
1							1
2							2
3							3
4							4
5							5
6							6
7							7
8							8
9							9
10							10
11							11
12							12
13							13
14							14
15							15

3.

GENERAL JOURNAL

PAGE

	DATE		DESCRIPTION	POST. REF.	DEBIT	CREDIT	
1							1
2							2
3							3
4							4
5							5
6							6
7							7
8							8
9							9
10							10
11							11
12							12
13							13
14							14
15							15

Problem 19-9A

1.

Problem 19-9A (Concluded)

2.

GENERAL JOURNAL

PAGE

DATE		DESCRIPTION	POST. REF.	DEBIT	CREDIT
1					
2					
3					
4					
5					
6					
7					
8					
9					
10					
11					
12					
13					
14					
15					
16					
17					
18					
19					
20					
21					
22					
23					
24					
25					
26					
27					
28					
29					
30					
31					
32					
33					
34					

Problem 19-10A

1.

Problem 19-10A (Concluded)

2.

GENERAL JOURNAL

PAGE

	DATE		DESCRIPTION	POST. REF.	DEBIT	CREDIT	
1							1
2							2
3							3
4							4
5							5
6							6
7							7
8							8
9							9
10							10
11							11
12							12
13							13
14							14
15							15
16							16
17							17
18							18
19							19
20							20
21							21
22							22
23							23
24							24
25							25
26							26
27							27
28							28
29							29
30							30
31							31
32							32
33							33
34							34

Exercise 19-1B

GENERAL JOURNAL

PAGE

	DATE		DESCRIPTION	POST. REF.	DEBIT	CREDIT	
1							1
2							2
3							3
4							4
5							5
6							6
7							7
8							8
9							9
10							10

Exercise 19-2B

Exercise 19-3B

1.

2.

Exercise 19-4B

1.

GENERAL JOURNAL PAGE

	DATE		DESCRIPTION	POST. REF.	DEBIT	CREDIT	
1							1
2							2
3							3
4							4
5							5
6							6
7							7
8							8
9							9
10							10

2.

Exercise 19-5B

GENERAL JOURNAL PAGE

	DATE		DESCRIPTION	POST. REF.	DEBIT	CREDIT	
1							1
2							2
3							3
4							4
5							5
6							6
7							7
8							8
9							9
10							10

Name ______________________

Problem 19-6B

GENERAL JOURNAL

PAGE

	DATE	DESCRIPTION	POST. REF.	DEBIT	CREDIT	
1						1
2						2
3						3
4						4
5						5
6						6
7						7
8						8
9						9
10						10
11						11
12						12
13						13
14						14
15						15
16						16
17						17
18						18
19						19
20						20
21						21
22						22
23						23
24						24
25						25
26						26
27						27
28						28
29						29
30						30
31						31
32						32
33						33
34						34
35						35

Problem 19-7B

1.

2.

Problem 19-7B (Concluded)

3.

GENERAL JOURNAL

PAGE

	DATE		DESCRIPTION	POST. REF.	DEBIT	CREDIT	
1							1
2							2
3							3
4							4
5							5
6							6
7							7
8							8
9							9
10							10
11							11
12							12
13							13
14							14
15							15
16							16
17							17
18							18

Problem 19-8B

1.

GENERAL JOURNAL

PAGE

	DATE		DESCRIPTION	POST. REF.	DEBIT	CREDIT	
1							1
2							2
3							3
4							4
5							5
6							6
7							7
8							8
9							9
10							10

Problem 19-8B (Concluded)

2.

GENERAL JOURNAL

PAGE

	DATE		DESCRIPTION	POST. REF.	DEBIT	CREDIT	
1							1
2							2
3							3
4							4
5							5
6							6
7							7
8							8
9							9
10							10
11							11
12							12
13							13
14							14
15							15

3.

GENERAL JOURNAL

PAGE

	DATE		DESCRIPTION	POST. REF.	DEBIT	CREDIT	
1							1
2							2
3							3
4							4
5							5
6							6
7							7
8							8
9							9
10							10
11							11
12							12
13							13
14							14
15							15

Problem 19-9B

1.

Problem 19-9B (Concluded)

2.

GENERAL JOURNAL

PAGE

DATE		DESCRIPTION	POST. REF.	DEBIT	CREDIT

Problem 19-10B

1.

Problem 19-10B (Concluded)
2.

GENERAL JOURNAL

PAGE

	DATE	DESCRIPTION	POST. REF.	DEBIT	CREDIT	
1						1
2						2
3						3
4						4
5						5
6						6
7						7
8						8
9						9
10						10
11						11
12						12
13						13
14						14
15						15
16						16
17						17
18						18
19						19
20						20
21						21
22						22
23						23
24						24
25						25
26						26
27						27
28						28
29						29
30						30
31						31
32						32
33						33
34						34

Mastery Problem

1.

GENERAL JOURNAL

PAGE

	DATE		DESCRIPTION	POST. REF.	DEBIT	CREDIT	
1							1
2							2
3							3
4							4
5							5
6							6
7							7
8							8
9							9
10							10
11							11
12							12
13							13
14							14
15							15
16							16
17							17
18							18
19							19
20							20
21							21
22							22
23							23
24							24
25							25
26							26
27							27
28							28
29							29
30							30
31							31
32							32
33							33
34							34

Mastery Problem (Continued)

2.

3.

GENERAL JOURNAL

PAGE

	DATE		DESCRIPTION	POST. REF.	DEBIT	CREDIT	
1							1
2							2
3							3
4							4
5							5
6							6
7							7
8							8
9							9
10							10
11							11

This page intentionally left blank.

Mastery Problem (Continued)

4.

Mastery Problem (Continued)

Mastery Problem (Continued)

GENERAL JOURNAL

PAGE

	DATE		DESCRIPTION	POST. REF.	DEBIT	CREDIT	
1							1
2							2
3							3
4							4
5							5
6							6
7							7
8							8
9							9
10							10
11							11
12							12
13							13
14							14
15							15
16							16
17							17
18							18
19							19
20							20
21							21
22							22
23							23
24							24
25							25
26							26
27							27
28							28
29							29
30							30
31							31
32							32
33							33
34							34
35							35
36							36

Mastery Problem (Concluded)

GENERAL JOURNAL PAGE

	DATE		DESCRIPTION	POST. REF.	DEBIT	CREDIT	
1							1
2							2
3							3
4							4
5							5
6							6
7							7
8							8
9							9
10							10
11							11
12							12
13							13
14							14
15							15
16							16

Challenge Problem

Comprehensive Problem 3: Specialized Accounting Procedures

1.

GENERAL JOURNAL

PAGE

	DATE		DESCRIPTION	POST. REF.	DEBIT	CREDIT	
1							1
2							2
3							3
4							4
5							5
6							6
7							7
8							8
9							9
10							10
11							11
12							12
13							13
14							14
15							15
16							16
17							17
18							18
19							19
20							20
21							21
22							22
23							23
24							24
25							25
26							26
27							27
28							28
29							29
30							30
31							31
32							32
33							33
34							34
35							35

Comprehensive Problem 3 (Continued)

GENERAL JOURNAL

PAGE

DATE	DESCRIPTION	POST. REF.	DEBIT	CREDIT

Comprehensive Problem 3 (Continued)

GENERAL JOURNAL

PAGE

	DATE		DESCRIPTION	POST. REF.	DEBIT	CREDIT	
1							1
2							2
3							3
4							4
5							5
6							6
7							7
8							8
9							9
10							10
11							11
12							12
13							13
14							14
15							15
16							16
17							17
18							18
19							19
20							20
21							21
22							22
23							23
24							24
25							25
26							26
27							27
28							28
29							29
30							30
31							31
32							32
33							33
34							34
35							35

Comprehensive Problem 3 (Continued)

GENERAL JOURNAL

PAGE

DATE	DESCRIPTION	POST. REF.	DEBIT	CREDIT

Comprehensive Problem 3 (Continued)

GENERAL JOURNAL

PAGE

DATE		DESCRIPTION	POST. REF.	DEBIT	CREDIT

Comprehensive Problem 3 (Continued)

GENERAL JOURNAL

PAGE

DATE		DESCRIPTION	POST. REF.	DEBIT	CREDIT

Comprehensive Problem 3 (Continued)

Use this space to estimate ending inventory.

Comprehensive Problem 3 (Continued)

2.

GENERAL JOURNAL

PAGE

DATE		DESCRIPTION	POST. REF.	DEBIT	CREDIT

Comprehensive Problem 3 (Continued)

GENERAL JOURNAL

PAGE

	DATE		DESCRIPTION	POST. REF.	DEBIT	CREDIT	
1							1
2							2
3							3
4							4
5							5
6							6
7							7
8							8
9							9
10							10
11							11
12							12
13							13
14							14
15							15
16							16
17							17
18							18
19							19
20							20
21							21
22							22
23							23
24							24
25							25
26							26
27							27
28							28
29							29
30							30
31							31
32							32
33							33
34							34
35							35

Comprehensive Problem 3 (Continued)

3.

Name ______________________________

Comprehensive Problem 3 (Continued)

4. and 5.

GENERAL JOURNAL

PAGE

	DATE		DESCRIPTION	POST. REF.	DEBIT	CREDIT	
1							1
2							2
3							3
4							4
5							5
6							6
7							7
8							8
9							9
10							10
11							11
12							12
13							13
14							14
15							15
16							16
17							17
18							18
19							19
20							20
21							21
22							22
23							23
24							24
25							25
26							26
27							27
28							28
29							29
30							30
31							31
32							32
33							33
34							34
35							35

Comprehensive Problem 3 (Concluded)

6.

GENERAL JOURNAL

PAGE

	DATE		DESCRIPTION	POST. REF.	DEBIT	CREDIT	
1							1
2							2
3							3
4							4
5							5
6							6
7							7
8							8
9							9
10							10
11							11
12							12
13							13
14							14
15							15
16							16
17							17
18							18
19							19
20							20
21							21
22							22
23							23
24							24
25							25
26							26
27							27
28							28
29							29
30							30
31							31
32							32
33							33
34							34
35							35

Exercise 20-1A

GENERAL JOURNAL PAGE

	DATE		DESCRIPTION	POST. REF.	DEBIT	CREDIT	
1							1
2							2
3							3
4							4
5							5
6							6
7							7
8							8
9							9
10							10
11							11
12							12
13							13
14							14
15							15

Exercise 20-2A

Situation 1

Exercise 20-2A (Concluded)
Situation 2

Name ______________________________

Exercise 20-3A

GENERAL JOURNAL

PAGE

DATE		DESCRIPTION	POST. REF.	DEBIT	CREDIT

Exercise 20-4A

GENERAL JOURNAL

PAGE

DATE		DESCRIPTION	POST. REF.	DEBIT	CREDIT

Name ______________________________

Exercise 20-5A

Problem 20-6A

1. **GENERAL JOURNAL** PAGE

DATE		DESCRIPTION	POST. REF.	DEBIT	CREDIT

Problem 20-6A (Concluded)

2.

Problem 20-7A

GENERAL JOURNAL

PAGE

DATE		DESCRIPTION	POST. REF.	DEBIT	CREDIT

Name ______________________________

Problem 20-8A

GENERAL JOURNAL

PAGE

	DATE		DESCRIPTION	POST. REF.	DEBIT	CREDIT	
1							1
2							2
3							3
4							4
5							5
6							6
7							7
8							8
9							9
10							10
11							11
12							12
13							13
14							14
15							15
16							16
17							17
18							18
19							19
20							20
21							21
22							22
23							23
24							24
25							25
26							26
27							27
28							28
29							29
30							30
31							31
32							32
33							33
34							34
35							35

Problem 20-9A

GENERAL JOURNAL

PAGE

DATE		DESCRIPTION	POST. REF.	DEBIT	CREDIT

Problem 20-9A (Concluded)

GENERAL JOURNAL

PAGE

DATE		DESCRIPTION	POST. REF.	DEBIT	CREDIT

Problem 20-10A

Exercise 20-1B

GENERAL JOURNAL PAGE

	DATE		DESCRIPTION	POST. REF.	DEBIT	CREDIT	
1							1
2							2
3							3
4							4
5							5
6							6
7							7
8							8
9							9
10							10
11							11
12							12
13							13
14							14
15							15

Exercise 20-2B

Situation 1

Exercise 20-2B (Concluded)

Situation 2

Exercise 20-3B

GENERAL JOURNAL

PAGE

	DATE		DESCRIPTION	POST. REF.	DEBIT	CREDIT	
1							1
2							2
3							3
4							4
5							5
6							6
7							7
8							8
9							9
10							10
11							11
12							12
13							13
14							14
15							15
16							16
17							17
18							18
19							19
20							20
21							21
22							22
23							23
24							24
25							25
26							26
27							27
28							28
29							29
30							30
31							31
32							32
33							33
34							34
35							35

Exercise 20-4B

GENERAL JOURNAL

PAGE

DATE		DESCRIPTION	POST. REF.	DEBIT	CREDIT

Name ________________________________

Exercise 20-5B

____

____

____

Problem 20-6B

1. **GENERAL JOURNAL** PAGE

DATE		DESCRIPTION	POST. REF.	DEBIT	CREDIT

Problem 20-6B (Concluded)

2.

Problem 20-7B

GENERAL JOURNAL

PAGE

DATE		DESCRIPTION	POST. REF.	DEBIT	CREDIT

Name ____________________

Problem 20-8B

GENERAL JOURNAL

PAGE

DATE		DESCRIPTION	POST. REF.	DEBIT	CREDIT

Problem 20-9B

GENERAL JOURNAL

PAGE

	DATE		DESCRIPTION	POST. REF.	DEBIT	CREDIT	
1							1
2							2
3							3
4							4
5							5
6							6
7							7
8							8
9							9
10							10
11							11
12							12
13							13
14							14
15							15
16							16
17							17
18							18
19							19
20							20
21							21
22							22
23							23
24							24
25							25
26							26
27							27
28							28
29							29
30							30
31							31
32							32
33							33
34							34
35							35

Problem 20-9B (Concluded)

GENERAL JOURNAL

PAGE

DATE		DESCRIPTION	POST. REF.	DEBIT	CREDIT

Problem 20-10B

Mastery Problem

1.

GENERAL JOURNAL

PAGE

DATE		DESCRIPTION	POST. REF.	DEBIT	CREDIT

Mastery Problem (Continued)

2.

Cash

Land

Common Stock Subscriptions Receivable

Preferred Stock Subscriptions Receivable

Common Stock Subscribed

Preferred Stock Subscribed

Common Stock

Preferred Stock

Paid-In Capital in Excess of Par—Common Stock

Paid-In Capital in Excess of Par—Preferred Stock

Paid-In Capital from Sale of Treasury Stock

Common Treasury Stock

Retained Earnings

Mastery Problem (Concluded)

3.

Challenge Problem

GENERAL JOURNAL

PAGE

DATE		DESCRIPTION	POST. REF.	DEBIT	CREDIT

Exercise 21-1A

1. and 2.

GENERAL JOURNAL PAGE

	DATE		DESCRIPTION	POST. REF.	DEBIT	CREDIT	
1							1
2							2
3							3
4							4
5							5
6							6
7							7
8							8
9							9
10							10
11							11
12							12
13							13
14							14

Exercise 21-2A

1.

GENERAL JOURNAL PAGE

	DATE		DESCRIPTION	POST. REF.	DEBIT	CREDIT	
1							1
2							2
3							3
4							4
5							5

2.

6							6
7							7
8							8
9							9
10							10
11							11
12							12
13							13
14							14

Exercise 21-3A

GENERAL JOURNAL

PAGE

	DATE		DESCRIPTION	POST. REF.	DEBIT	CREDIT	
1							1
2							2
3							3
4							4
5							5
6							6
7							7
8							8
9							9
10							10
11							11
12							12
13							13
14							14
15							15

Exercise 21-4A

1. and 2.

GENERAL JOURNAL

PAGE

	DATE		DESCRIPTION	POST. REF.	DEBIT	CREDIT	
1							1
2							2
3							3
4							4
5							5
6							6
7							7
8							8
9							9
10							10
11							11
12							12
13							13
14							14
15							15

Exercise 21-5A

GENERAL JOURNAL PAGE

	DATE		DESCRIPTION	POST. REF.	DEBIT	CREDIT	
1							1
2							2
3							3
4							4
5							5
6							6
7							7

Exercise 21-6A

GENERAL JOURNAL PAGE

	DATE		DESCRIPTION	POST. REF.	DEBIT	CREDIT	
1							1
2							2
3							3
4							4
5							5
6							6
7							7
8							8

Exercise 21-7A

Problem 21-8A

GENERAL JOURNAL

PAGE

	DATE		DESCRIPTION	POST. REF.	DEBIT	CREDIT	
1							1
2							2
3							3
4							4
5							5
6							6
7							7
8							8
9							9
10							10
11							11
12							12
13							13
14							14
15							15
16							16
17							17
18							18
19							19
20							20
21							21
22							22
23							23
24							24
25							25
26							26
27							27
28							28
29							29
30							30
31							31
32							32
33							33
34							34
35							35

Problem 21-9A

GENERAL JOURNAL

PAGE

	DATE		DESCRIPTION	POST. REF.	DEBIT	CREDIT	
1							1
2							2
3							3
4							4
5							5
6							6
7							7
8							8
9							9
10							10
11							11
12							12
13							13
14							14
15							15
16							16
17							17
18							18
19							19
20							20
21							21
22							22
23							23
24							24
25							25
26							26
27							27
28							28
29							29
30							30
31							31
32							32
33							33
34							34
35							35

Problem 21-10A

GENERAL JOURNAL PAGE

	DATE		DESCRIPTION	POST. REF.	DEBIT	CREDIT	
1							1
2							2
3							3
4							4
5							5
6							6
7							7
8							8
9							9
10							10
11							11
12							12
13							13
14							14
15							15
16							16
17							17
18							18
19							19
20							20

Problem 21-11A

1.

GENERAL JOURNAL PAGE

	DATE		DESCRIPTION	POST. REF.	DEBIT	CREDIT	
1							1
2							2
3							3
4							4
5							5
6							6
7							7
8							8
9							9
10							10

Problem 21-11A (Continued)

GENERAL JOURNAL

PAGE

	DATE		DESCRIPTION	POST. REF.	DEBIT	CREDIT	
1							1
2							2
3							3
4							4
5							5
6							6
7							7
8							8
9							9
10							10
11							11
12							12
13							13
14							14
15							15
16							16
17							17
18							18
19							19
20							20
21							21
22							22
23							23
24							24
25							25
26							26

2.

Retained Earnings—Appropriated for Land Acquisition	
	Bal. 60,000

Retained Earnings—Unappropriated	
	Bal. 900,000

Problem 21-11A (Concluded)

3.

Exercise 21-1B

1. and 2.

GENERAL JOURNAL PAGE

	DATE		DESCRIPTION	POST. REF.	DEBIT	CREDIT	
1							1
2							2
3							3
4							4
5							5
6							6
7							7
8							8
9							9
10							10
11							11
12							12
13							13
14							14

Exercise 21-2B

1.

GENERAL JOURNAL PAGE

	DATE		DESCRIPTION	POST. REF.	DEBIT	CREDIT	
1							1
2							2
3							3
4							4
5							5

2.

6							6
7							7
8							8
9							9
10							10
11							11
12							12
13							13
14							14

Exercise 21-3B

GENERAL JOURNAL PAGE

	DATE		DESCRIPTION	POST. REF.	DEBIT	CREDIT	
1							1
2							2
3							3
4							4
5							5
6							6
7							7
8							8
9							9
10							10
11							11
12							12
13							13
14							14
15							15

Exercise 21-4B

1. and 2.

GENERAL JOURNAL PAGE

	DATE		DESCRIPTION	POST. REF.	DEBIT	CREDIT	
1							1
2							2
3							3
4							4
5							5
6							6
7							7
8							8
9							9
10							10
11							11
12							12
13							13
14							14
15							15

Exercise 21-5B

GENERAL JOURNAL PAGE

	DATE		DESCRIPTION	POST. REF.	DEBIT	CREDIT	
1							1
2							2
3							3
4							4
5							5
6							6
7							7
8							8

Exercise 21-6B

GENERAL JOURNAL PAGE

	DATE		DESCRIPTION	POST. REF.	DEBIT	CREDIT	
1							1
2							2
3							3
4							4
5							5
6							6
7							7
8							8

Exercise 21-7B

Problem 21-8B

GENERAL JOURNAL

PAGE

DATE		DESCRIPTION	POST. REF.	DEBIT	CREDIT

Problem 21-9B

GENERAL JOURNAL

PAGE

DATE		DESCRIPTION	POST. REF.	DEBIT	CREDIT	
1						1
2						2
3						3
4						4
5						5
6						6
7						7
8						8
9						9
10						10
11						11
12						12
13						13
14						14
15						15
16						16
17						17
18						18
19						19
20						20
21						21
22						22
23						23
24						24
25						25
26						26
27						27
28						28
29						29
30						30
31						31
32						32
33						33
34						34
35						35

Problem 21-10B

GENERAL JOURNAL PAGE

	DATE		DESCRIPTION	POST. REF.	DEBIT	CREDIT	
1							1
2							2
3							3
4							4
5							5
6							6
7							7
8							8
9							9
10							10
11							11
12							12
13							13
14							14
15							15
16							16
17							17
18							18
19							19
20							20

Problem 21-11B

1.

GENERAL JOURNAL PAGE

	DATE		DESCRIPTION	POST. REF.	DEBIT	CREDIT	
1							1
2							2
3							3
4							4
5							5
6							6
7							7
8							8
9							9
10							10

Problem 21-11B (Continued)

GENERAL JOURNAL

PAGE

	DATE	DESCRIPTION	POST. REF.	DEBIT	CREDIT	
1						1
2						2
3						3
4						4
5						5
6						6
7						7
8						8
9						9
10						10
11						11
12						12
13						13
14						14
15						15
16						16
17						17
18						18
19						19
20						20
21						21
22						22
23						23
24						24
25						25
26						26

2.

Retained Earnings—Appropriated for Land Acquisition	
	Bal. 75,000

Retained Earnings—Unappropriated	
	Bal. 825,000

Problem 21-11B (Concluded)

3.

Mastery Problem

1.

GENERAL JOURNAL

PAGE

DATE		DESCRIPTION	POST. REF.	DEBIT	CREDIT

Mastery Problem (Concluded)

2.

Retained Earnings—Appropriated	
	Bal. 50,000

Retained Earnings—Unappropriated	
	Bal. 800,000

3.

Challenge Problem

1.

GENERAL JOURNAL

PAGE

	DATE		DESCRIPTION	POST. REF.	DEBIT	CREDIT	
1							1
2							2
3							3
4							4
5							5
6							6
7							7
8							8
9							9
10							10
11							11
12							12
13							13
14							14
15							15
16							16
17							17
18							18
19							19
20							20
21							21
22							22

2.

(a)

(b)

Exercise 22-1A

GENERAL JOURNAL

PAGE

	DATE		DESCRIPTION	POST. REF.	DEBIT	CREDIT	
1							1
2							2
3							3
4							4
5							5
6							6
7							7
8							8
9							9
10							10
11							11
12							12
13							13
14							14

Exercise 22-2A

GENERAL JOURNAL

PAGE

	DATE		DESCRIPTION	POST. REF.	DEBIT	CREDIT	
1							1
2							2
3							3
4							4
5							5
6							6
7							7
8							8
9							9
10							10
11							11
12							12
13							13
14							14
15							15

Exercise 22-3A

GENERAL JOURNAL

PAGE

DATE		DESCRIPTION	POST. REF.	DEBIT	CREDIT

Exercise 22-4A

GENERAL JOURNAL

PAGE

DATE		DESCRIPTION	POST. REF.	DEBIT	CREDIT

Exercise 22-5A

GENERAL JOURNAL PAGE

	DATE		DESCRIPTION	POST. REF.	DEBIT	CREDIT	
1							1
2							2
3							3
4							4
5							5
6							6
7							7
8							8
9							9
10							10
11							11
12							12
13							13
14							14

Exercise 22-6A

GENERAL JOURNAL PAGE

	DATE		DESCRIPTION	POST. REF.	DEBIT	CREDIT	
1							1
2							2
3							3
4							4
5							5
6							6
7							7
8							8
9							9
10							10
11							11
12							12
13							13
14							14

Exercise 22-7A

GENERAL JOURNAL

PAGE

DATE		DESCRIPTION	POST. REF.	DEBIT	CREDIT

Problem 22-8A

GENERAL JOURNAL

PAGE

	DATE	DESCRIPTION	POST. REF.	DEBIT	CREDIT	
1						1
2						2
3						3
4						4
5						5
6						6
7						7
8						8
9						9
10						10
11						11
12						12
13						13
14						14
15						15
16						16
17						17
18						18
19						19
20						20
21						21
22						22
23						23
24						24
25						25
26						26
27						27
28						28
29						29
30						30
31						31
32						32
33						33
34						34
35						35

Problem 22-9A

1.

GENERAL JOURNAL

PAGE

	DATE		DESCRIPTION	POST. REF.	DEBIT	CREDIT	
1							1
2							2
3							3
4							4
5							5
6							6
7							7
8							8
9							9
10							10
11							11
12							12
13							13
14							14
15							15
16							16
17							17
18							18
19							19
20							20
21							21
22							22
23							23
24							24
25							25
26							26
27							27
28							28
29							29
30							30
31							31
32							32
33							33
34							34
35							35

Problem 22-9A (Concluded)

2.

3.

Problem 22-10A

1.

GENERAL JOURNAL PAGE

	DATE		DESCRIPTION	POST. REF.	DEBIT	CREDIT	
1							1
2							2
3							3
4							4
5							5
6							6
7							7
8							8
9							9
10							10
11							11
12							12
13							13
14							14
15							15
16							16
17							17

Problem 22-10A (Concluded)

GENERAL JOURNAL

PAGE

	DATE		DESCRIPTION	POST. REF.	DEBIT	CREDIT	
1							1
2							2
3							3
4							4
5							5
6							6
7							7
8							8
9							9
10							10
11							11
12							12
13							13
14							14
15							15
16							16
17							17
18							18
19							19
20							20

2.

Problem 22-11A

GENERAL JOURNAL

PAGE

DATE		DESCRIPTION	POST. REF.	DEBIT	CREDIT

Problem 22-12A

GENERAL JOURNAL

PAGE

	DATE		DESCRIPTION	POST. REF.	DEBIT	CREDIT	
1							1
2							2
3							3
4							4
5							5
6							6
7							7
8							8
9							9
10							10
11							11
12							12
13							13
14							14
15							15
16							16
17							17
18							18
19							19
20							20
21							21
22							22
23							23
24							24
25							25
26							26
27							27
28							28
29							29
30							30
31							31
32							32
33							33
34							34
35							35

Problem 22-13A

GENERAL JOURNAL

PAGE

	DATE		DESCRIPTION	POST. REF.	DEBIT	CREDIT	
1							1
2							2
3							3
4							4
5							5
6							6
7							7
8							8
9							9
10							10
11							11
12							12
13							13
14							14
15							15
16							16
17							17
18							18
19							19
20							20
21							21
22							22
23							23
24							24
25							25
26							26
27							27
28							28
29							29
30							30
31							31
32							32
33							33
34							34
35							35

Exercise 22-1B

GENERAL JOURNAL

PAGE

	DATE		DESCRIPTION	POST. REF.	DEBIT	CREDIT	
1							1
2							2
3							3
4							4
5							5
6							6
7							7
8							8
9							9
10							10
11							11
12							12
13							13
14							14

Exercise 22-2B

GENERAL JOURNAL

PAGE

	DATE		DESCRIPTION	POST. REF.	DEBIT	CREDIT	
1							1
2							2
3							3
4							4
5							5
6							6
7							7
8							8
9							9
10							10
11							11
12							12
13							13
14							14
15							15
16							16

Exercise 22-3B

GENERAL JOURNAL PAGE

	DATE		DESCRIPTION	POST. REF.	DEBIT	CREDIT	
1							1
2							2
3							3
4							4
5							5
6							6
7							7
8							8
9							9
10							10
11							11
12							12
13							13
14							14
15							15

Exercise 22-4B

GENERAL JOURNAL PAGE

	DATE		DESCRIPTION	POST. REF.	DEBIT	CREDIT	
1							1
2							2
3							3
4							4
5							5
6							6
7							7
8							8
9							9
10							10
11							11
12							12
13							13
14							14
15							15

Exercise 22-5B

GENERAL JOURNAL PAGE

	DATE		DESCRIPTION	POST. REF.	DEBIT	CREDIT	
1							1
2							2
3							3
4							4
5							5
6							6
7							7
8							8
9							9
10							10
11							11
12							12
13							13
14							14
15							15

Exercise 22-6B

GENERAL JOURNAL PAGE

	DATE		DESCRIPTION	POST. REF.	DEBIT	CREDIT	
1							1
2							2
3							3
4							4
5							5
6							6
7							7
8							8
9							9
10							10
11							11
12							12
13							13
14							14
15							15

Exercise 22-7B

GENERAL JOURNAL PAGE

	DATE		DESCRIPTION	POST. REF.	DEBIT	CREDIT	
1							1
2							2
3							3
4							4
5							5
6							6
7							7
8							8
9							9
10							10
11							11

Problem 22-8B

GENERAL JOURNAL PAGE

	DATE		DESCRIPTION	POST. REF.	DEBIT	CREDIT	
1							1
2							2
3							3
4							4
5							5
6							6
7							7
8							8
9							9
10							10
11							11
12							12
13							13
14							14
15							15
16							16
17							17
18							18
19							19
20							20
21							21
22							22

Problem 22-9B

1.

GENERAL JOURNAL

PAGE

	DATE	DESCRIPTION	POST. REF.	DEBIT	CREDIT	
1						1
2						2
3						3
4						4
5						5
6						6
7						7
8						8
9						9
10						10
11						11
12						12
13						13
14						14
15						15
16						16
17						17
18						18
19						19
20						20
21						21
22						22
23						23
24						24
25						25
26						26
27						27
28						28
29						29
30						30
31						31
32						32
33						33
34						34
35						35

Problem 22-9B (Concluded)

2.

Problem 22-10B

1.

GENERAL JOURNAL PAGE

	DATE		DESCRIPTION	POST. REF.	DEBIT	CREDIT	
1							1
2							2
3							3
4							4
5							5
6							6
7							7
8							8
9							9
10							10
11							11
12							12
13							13
14							14
15							15
16							16
17							17
18							18
19							19
20							20

Problem 22-10B (Concluded)

GENERAL JOURNAL

PAGE

	DATE		DESCRIPTION	POST. REF.	DEBIT	CREDIT	
1							1
2							2
3							3
4							4
5							5
6							6
7							7
8							8
9							9
10							10
11							11
12							12

2.

3.

Name ____________________________

Problem 22-11B

GENERAL JOURNAL

PAGE

DATE		DESCRIPTION	POST. REF.	DEBIT	CREDIT

Problem 22-12B

GENERAL JOURNAL

PAGE

	DATE	DESCRIPTION	POST. REF.	DEBIT	CREDIT	
1						1
2						2
3						3
4						4
5						5
6						6
7						7
8						8
9						9
10						10
11						11
12						12
13						13
14						14
15						15
16						16
17						17
18						18
19						19
20						20
21						21
22						22
23						23
24						24
25						25
26						26
27						27
28						28
29						29
30						30
31						31
32						32
33						33
34						34
35						35

Problem 22-13B

GENERAL JOURNAL

PAGE

	DATE		DESCRIPTION	POST. REF.	DEBIT	CREDIT	
1							1
2							2
3							3
4							4
5							5
6							6
7							7
8							8
9							9
10							10
11							11
12							12
13							13
14							14
15							15
16							16
17							17
18							18
19							19
20							20
21							21
22							22
23							23
24							24
25							25
26							26
27							27
28							28
29							29
30							30
31							31
32							32
33							33
34							34
35							35

Mastery Problem

1.

GENERAL JOURNAL

PAGE

DATE		DESCRIPTION	POST. REF.	DEBIT	CREDIT

Mastery Problem (Concluded)

GENERAL JOURNAL

PAGE

	DATE		DESCRIPTION	POST. REF.	DEBIT	CREDIT	
1							1
2							2
3							3
4							4
5							5
6							6
7							7
8							8
9							9
10							10
11							11
12							12
13							13
14							14
15							15

2.

Challenge Problem

1.

2.

GENERAL JOURNAL PAGE

	DATE		DESCRIPTION	POST. REF.	DEBIT	CREDIT	
1							1
2							2
3							3
4							4
5							5
6							6
7							7
8							8
9							9
10							10
11							11
12							12
13							13
14							14
15							15
16							16
17							17
18							18
19							19
20							20

APPENDIX: EFFECTIVE INTEREST METHOD

Exercise 22Apx-1A

GENERAL JOURNAL PAGE

	DATE		DESCRIPTION	POST. REF.	DEBIT	CREDIT	
1							1
2							2
3							3
4							4
5							5
6							6

Problem 22Apx-2A

GENERAL JOURNAL PAGE

	DATE		DESCRIPTION	POST. REF.	DEBIT	CREDIT	
1							1
2							2
3							3
4							4
5							5
6							6
7							7
8							8
9							9
10							10
11							11
12							12
13							13
14							14
15							15
16							16
17							17
18							18
19							19
20							20

Exercise 22Apx-1B

GENERAL JOURNAL PAGE

DATE		DESCRIPTION	POST. REF.	DEBIT	CREDIT

Problem 22Apx-2B

GENERAL JOURNAL PAGE

DATE		DESCRIPTION	POST. REF.	DEBIT	CREDIT

Exercise 23-1A

a. ______________ g. ______________

b. ______________ h. ______________

c. ______________ i. ______________

d. ______________ j. ______________

e. ______________ k. ______________

f. ______________ l. ______________

Exercise 23-2A

Exercise 23-3A

Exercise 23-4A

Exercise 23-5A

Exercise 23-6A

Exercise 23-7A

Exercise 23-8A

Cash		Accrued Interest Payable		Interest Expense	

Problem 23-9A

Name ______________________________

Problem 23-10A

Problem 23-11A

Problem 23-12A

T Accounts for Indirect Method Statement of Cash Flows
McDowell Company

Accrued Interest Receivable

BB 610	
EB 720	

Notes Payable

	102,000 BB
	118,000 EB

Common Stock

	800,000 BB
	900,000 EB

Accounts Receivable

BB 325,800	
EB 310,700	

Accounts Payable

	195,000 BB
	110,000 EB

Paid-In Capital in Excess of Par—Common Stock

	390,000 BB
	430,000 EB

Merchandise Inventory

BB 540,200	
EB 685,400	

Income Tax Payable

	25,000 BB
	20,000 EB

Retained Earnings

	360,000 BB
	532,710 EB

Supplies and Prepayments

BB 39,000	
EB 27,000	

Accrued and Withheld Payroll Taxes

	14,900 BB
	16,400 EB

Store Equipment

BB 460,000	
EB 470,000	

Accrued Interest Payable

	1,035 BB
	875 EB

Accumulated Depreciation—Store Equipment

	150,000 BB
	180,000 EB

Office Equipment

BB 400,000	
EB 430,000	

Accumulated Depreciation—Office Equipment

	76,000 BB
	88,000 EB

Delivery Equipment

BB 390,000	
EB 530,000	

Accumulated Depreciation—Delivery Equipment

	100,000 BB
	140,000 EB

BB: Beginning Balance
EB: Ending Balance

Problem 23-12A (Concluded)

Exercise 23-1B

a. ____________________ g. ____________________

b. ____________________ h. ____________________

c. ____________________ i. ____________________

d. ____________________ j. ____________________

e. ____________________ k. ____________________

f. ____________________ l. ____________________

Exercise 23-2B

Exercise 23-3B

Exercise 23-4B

Exercise 23-5B

Exercise 23-6B

Exercise 23-7B

Exercise 23-8B

Cash	

Accrued Interest Payable	

Interest Expense	

Problem 23-9B

Problem 23-10B

Problem 23-11B

Problem 23-12B

T Accounts for Indirect Method Statement of Cash Flows
McGinnis Company

Accrued Interest Receivable

BB	580		
EB	830		

Notes Payable

		109,000	BB
		117,000	EB

Common Stock

		700,000	BB
		800,000	EB

Accounts Receivable

BB	309,200		
EB	300,600		

Accounts Payable

		185,000	BB
		135,000	EB

Paid-In Capital in Excess of Par—Common Stock

		380,000	BB
		500,000	EB

Merchandise Inventory

BB	495,800		
EB	580,300		

Income Tax Payable

		15,000	BB
		25,000	EB

Retained Earnings

		320,000	BB
		471,350	EB

Supplies and Prepayments

BB	32,000		
EB	65,000		

Accrued and Withheld Payroll Taxes

		13,400	BB
		15,800	EB

Store Equipment

BB	420,000		
EB	560,000		

Accrued Interest Payable

		1,200	BB
		900	EB

Accumulated Depreciation—Store Equipment

		90,000	BB
		120,000	EB

Office Equipment

BB	380,000		
EB	320,000		

Accumulated Depreciation—Office Equipment

		100,500	BB
		30,500	EB

Delivery Equipment

BB	330,000		
EB	430,000		

Accumulated Depreciation—Delivery Equipment

		120,000	BB
		150,000	EB

BB: Beginning Balance
EB: Ending Balance

Problem 23-12B (Concluded)

Mastery Problem

T Accounts for Indirect Method Statement of Cash Flows
Peachfield Corporation

Accrued Interest Receivable

BB	250	
EB	320	

Accounts Receivable

BB	140,905	
EB	152,945	

Merchandise Inventory

BB	295,400	
EB	355,490	

Supplies and Prepayments

BB	21,500	
EB	14,500	

Store Equipment

BB	232,800	
EB	308,000	

Delivery Equipment

BB	192,000	
EB	270,000	

Accumulated Depreciation—Delivery Equipment

	48,000	BB
	75,000	EB

Office Equipment

BB	203,940	
EB	148,000	

Accumulated Depreciation—Office Equipment

	36,600	BB
	38,000	EB

Notes Payable

	54,780	BB
	65,480	EB

Accounts Payable

	125,473	BB
	53,500	EB

Income Tax Payable

	5,000	BB
	7,000	EB

Accrued and Withheld Payroll Taxes

	7,644	BB
	8,760	EB

Accumulated Depreciation—Store Equipment

	84,000	BB
	108,000	EB

Common Stock

	388,000	BB
	500,000	EB

Paid-In Capital in Excess of Par—Common Stock

	234,000	BB
	240,000	EB

Retained Earnings

	141,973	BB
	238,737	EB

Accrued Interest Payable

	525	BB
	450	EB

Long-Term Notes Payable

	—	BB
	20,000	EB

BB: Beginning Balance
EB: Ending Balance

Mastery Problem (Concluded)

Challenge Problem

Exercise 23Apx-1A

Cash		Accounts Receivable		Sales	

Exercise 23Apx-2A

Cash		Merchandise Inventory		Accounts Payable		Cost of Goods Sold	

Exercise 23Apx-3A

Exercise 23Apx-4A

Problem 23Apx-5A

1.

Income Statement	Additions	Deductions	Cash Flows

2.

Problem 23Apx-6A

1.

Income Statement	Additions	Deductions	Cash Flows

Problem 23Apx-6A (Concluded)

2.

Name ______________________________

Problem 23Apx-7A

1.

____

____

____

Income Statement	Additions	Deductions	Cash Flows

Problem 23Apx-7A (Concluded)

2.

Exercise 23Apx-1B

Cash	Accounts Receivable	Sales

Exercise 23Apx-2B

Cash	Merchandise Inventory	Accounts Payable	Cost of Goods Sold

Exercise 23Apx-3B

Exercise 23Apx-4B

Problem 23Apx-5B

1.

Income Statement	Additions	Deductions	Cash Flows

2.

Problem 23Apx-6B

1.

Income Statement	Additions	Deductions	Cash Flows

Problem 23Apx-6B (Concluded)

2.

Problem 23Apx-7B

1.

Income Statement	Additions	Deductions	Cash Flows

Problem 23Apx-7B (Concluded)

2.

Exercise 24-1A

Exercise 24-2A

Exercise 24-3A

Exercise 24-4A

Exercise 24-5A

Exercise 24-6A

Exercise 24-7A

Problem 24-8A

	AMOUNT	AMOUNT	AMOUNT	PERCENT

Problem 24-8A (Concluded)

	AMOUNT	AMOUNT	AMOUNT	PERCENT

Problem 24-9A

	AMOUNT	PERCENT	AMOUNT	PERCENT

Name ______________________________

Problem 24-9A (Concluded)

	AMOUNT	PERCENT	AMOUNT	PERCENT

Problem 24-10A

Problem 24-10A (Concluded)

Exercise 24-1B

Exercise 24-2B

Exercise 24-3B

Exercise 24-4B

Exercise 24-5B

Exercise 24-6B

Exercise 24-7B

Problem 24-8B

	AMOUNT	AMOUNT	AMOUNT	PERCENT

Problem 24-8B (Concluded)

	AMOUNT	AMOUNT	AMOUNT	PERCENT

Problem 24-9B

	AMOUNT	PERCENT	AMOUNT	PERCENT

Problem 24-9B (Concluded)

	AMOUNT	PERCENT	AMOUNT	PERCENT

Problem 24-10B

Problem 24-10B (Concluded)

Name ________________________________

Mastery Problem

1.

	AMOUNT	AMOUNT	AMOUNT	PERCENT

Mastery Problem (Continued)

	AMOUNT	AMOUNT	AMOUNT	PERCENT

Mastery Problem (Continued)

	AMOUNT	AMOUNT	AMOUNT	PERCENT

Mastery Problem (Continued)

2.

	AMOUNT	PERCENT	AMOUNT	PERCENT

Mastery Problem (Continued)

	AMOUNT	PERCENT	AMOUNT	PERCENT

Mastery Problem (Continued)

	AMOUNT	PERCENT	AMOUNT	PERCENT

Mastery Problem (Continued)

3.

Mastery Problem (Continued)

4.

Mastery Problem (Continued)

5.

Mastery Problem (Concluded)

6.

7.

Challenge Problem

Challenge Problem (Concluded)

Exercise 25-1A

Exercise 25-2A

Exercise 25-3A

Exercise 25-4A

Name ______________________________

Exercise 25-5A

	Dept. A	Dept. B

Exercise 25-6A

	Dept. A	Dept. B

Problem 25-7A

1.

	COMMERCIAL SALES	INDUSTRIAL SALES	TOTAL

2.

Problem 25-8A

1.

2.

Problem 25-9A

1.

2.

Problem 25-10A

1.

Williams and Lloyd Company

	Dept. A	Dept. B	Dept. C	Total
Net sales	$380,000	$260,000	$290,000	$930,000
Cost of goods sold	210,000	140,000	160,000	510,000
Gross profit	$170,000	$120,000	$130,000	$420,000
Direct operating expenses	100,000	90,000	80,000	270,000
Departmental direct operating margin	$ 70,000	$ 30,000	$ 50,000	$150,000
Indirect operating expenses	40,000	35,000	40,000	115,000
Operating income (loss)	$ 30,000	$ (5,000)	$ 10,000	$ 35,000

2.

Exercise 25-1B

Exercise 25-2B

Exercise 25-3B

Exercise 25-4B

Exercise 25-5B

	Dept. A	Dept. B

Exercise 25-6B

	Dept. A	Dept. B

Problem 25-7B

1.

	RETAIL SALES	WHOLESALE SALES	TOTAL

2.

Problem 25-8B

1.

2.

Name ______________________________

Problem 25-9B

1.

2.

Problem 25-10B

1.

Mueller and Kenington Company

	Dept. A	Dept. B	Dept. C	Total
Net sales	$680,000	$730,000	$690,000	$2,100,000
Cost of goods sold	400,000	380,000	360,000	1,140,000
Gross profit	$280,000	$350,000	$330,000	$ 960,000
Direct operating expenses	230,000	240,000	210,000	680,000
Departmental direct operating margin	$ 50,000	$110,000	$120,000	$ 280,000
Indirect operating expenses	70,000	70,000	70,000	210,000
Operating income (loss)	$ (20,000)	$ 40,000	$ 50,000	$ 70,000

2.

Mastery Problem

1. a.

b.

Mastery Problem (Continued)

2. a.

b.

Mastery Problem (Concluded)

3.

Challenge Problem

Name ______________________________

Exercise 26-1A

Exercise 26-2A

Exercise 26-3A

GENERAL JOURNAL

PAGE

	DATE		DESCRIPTION	POST. REF.	DEBIT	CREDIT	
1							1
2							2
3							3
4							4
5							5
6							6
7							7
8							8
9							9
10							10
11							11
12							12
13							13
14							14
15							15
16							16
17							17
18							18
19							19
20							20
21							21
22							22
23							23
24							24
25							25
26							26
27							27
28							28
29							29
30							30
31							31
32							32
33							33
34							34
35							35

Exercise 26-4A

GENERAL JOURNAL

PAGE

	DATE		DESCRIPTION	POST. REF.	DEBIT	CREDIT	
1							1
2							2
3							3
4							4
5							5
6							6
7							7
8							8
9							9
10							10
11							11
12							12
13							13
14							14
15							15
16							16
17							17
18							18
19							19
20							20
21							21
22							22
23							23
24							24
25							25
26							26
27							27
28							28
29							29
30							30
31							31
32							32
33							33
34							34
35							35

Exercise 26-5A

(1)

(2)

(3)

Exercise 26-6A

GENERAL JOURNAL

PAGE

DATE		DESCRIPTION	POST. REF.	DEBIT	CREDIT

Exercise 26-6A (Concluded)

GENERAL JOURNAL

PAGE

DATE	DESCRIPTION	POST. REF.	DEBIT	CREDIT

Problem 26-7A

1.

2.

Problem 26-8A

GENERAL JOURNAL

PAGE

	DATE		DESCRIPTION	POST. REF.	DEBIT	CREDIT	
1							1
2							2
3							3
4							4
5							5
6							6
7							7
8							8
9							9
10							10
11							11
12							12
13							13
14							14
15							15
16							16
17							17
18							18
19							19
20							20
21							21
22							22
23							23
24							24
25							25
26							26
27							27
28							28
29							29
30							30
31							31
32							32
33							33
34							34
35							35

Problem 26-9A

1.

GENERAL JOURNAL

PAGE

	DATE		DESCRIPTION	POST. REF.	DEBIT	CREDIT	
1							1
2							2
3							3
4							4
5							5
6							6
7							7
8							8
9							9
10							10
11							11
12							12
13							13
14							14
15							15
16							16
17							17
18							18
19							19
20							20
21							21
22							22
23							23
24							24
25							25
26							26
27							27
28							28
29							29
30							30
31							31
32							32
33							33
34							34
35							35

Name ____________________

Problem 26-9A (Continued)

GENERAL JOURNAL

PAGE

DATE		DESCRIPTION	POST. REF.	DEBIT	CREDIT

Problem 26-9A (Concluded)

2.

Work in Process	

Finished Goods	

Problem 26-10A

1. **GENERAL JOURNAL** PAGE

	DATE	DESCRIPTION	POST. REF.	DEBIT	CREDIT	
1						1
2						2
3						3
4						4
5						5
6						6
7						7
8						8
9						9
10						10
11						11
12						12
13						13
14						14
15						15
16						16
17						17
18						18
19						19
20						20
21						21
22						22

Problem 26-10A (Continued)

GENERAL JOURNAL

PAGE

	DATE		DESCRIPTION	POST. REF.	DEBIT	CREDIT	
1							1
2							2
3							3
4							4
5							5
6							6
7							7
8							8
9							9
10							10
11							11
12							12
13							13
14							14
15							15
16							16
17							17
18							18
19							19
20							20
21							21
22							22
23							23
24							24
25							25
26							26
27							27
28							28
29							29
30							30
31							31
32							32
33							33
34							34
35							35
36							36

Problem 26-10A (Concluded)

2.

Work in Process	

Finished Goods	

3.

Name ____________________

Exercise 26-1B

Exercise 26-2B

Name ______________________________

Exercise 26-3B

GENERAL JOURNAL

PAGE

DATE		DESCRIPTION	POST. REF.	DEBIT	CREDIT

Exercise 26-4B

GENERAL JOURNAL

PAGE

DATE		DESCRIPTION	POST. REF.	DEBIT	CREDIT

Exercise 26-5B

(1)

(2)

(3)

Exercise 26-6B

GENERAL JOURNAL

PAGE

DATE	DESCRIPTION	POST. REF.	DEBIT	CREDIT

Name ______________________________

Exercise 26-6B (Concluded)

GENERAL JOURNAL

PAGE

	DATE		DESCRIPTION	POST. REF.	DEBIT	CREDIT	
1							1
2							2
3							3
4							4
5							5
6							6
7							7
8							8
9							9
10							10
11							11
12							12
13							13
14							14
15							15
16							16
17							17
18							18
19							19
20							20
21							21
22							22
23							23
24							24
25							25
26							26
27							27
28							28
29							29
30							30
31							31
32							32
33							33
34							34
35							35
36							36

Problem 26-7B

1.

2.

Name ______________________________

Problem 26-8B

GENERAL JOURNAL

PAGE

DATE		DESCRIPTION	POST. REF.	DEBIT	CREDIT

Problem 26-9B

1.

GENERAL JOURNAL

PAGE

DATE		DESCRIPTION	POST. REF.	DEBIT	CREDIT

Problem 26-9B (Continued)

GENERAL JOURNAL

PAGE

DATE		DESCRIPTION	POST. REF.	DEBIT	CREDIT

Problem 26-9B (Concluded)

2.

Work in Process	

Finished Goods	

Problem 26-10B

1. GENERAL JOURNAL PAGE

	DATE		DESCRIPTION	POST. REF.	DEBIT	CREDIT	
1							1
2							2
3							3
4							4
5							5
6							6
7							7
8							8
9							9
10							10
11							11
12							12
13							13
14							14
15							15
16							16
17							17
18							18
19							19
20							20
21							21

Problem 26-10B (Continued)

GENERAL JOURNAL

PAGE

	DATE		DESCRIPTION	POST. REF.	DEBIT	CREDIT	
1							1
2							2
3							3
4							4
5							5
6							6
7							7
8							8
9							9
10							10
11							11
12							12
13							13
14							14
15							15
16							16
17							17
18							18
19							19
20							20
21							21
22							22
23							23
24							24
25							25
26							26
27							27
28							28
29							29
30							30
31							31
32							32
33							33
34							34
35							35
36							36

Problem 26-10B (Concluded)

2.

Work in Process		Finished Goods	

3.

Mastery Problem

1.

GENERAL JOURNAL

PAGE

	DATE		DESCRIPTION	POST. REF.	DEBIT	CREDIT	
1							1
2							2
3							3
4							4
5							5
6							6
7							7
8							8
9							9
10							10
11							11
12							12
13							13
14							14
15							15
16							16
17							17
18							18
19							19
20							20
21							21
22							22
23							23
24							24
25							25
26							26
27							27
28							28
29							29
30							30
31							31
32							32
33							33
34							34
35							35

Mastery Problem (Continued)

GENERAL JOURNAL

PAGE

DATE		DESCRIPTION	POST. REF.	DEBIT	CREDIT

Mastery Problem (Concluded)

2.

Work in Process	

Finished Goods	

3.

____

____

____

____

____

____

4.

Factory Overhead	

Challenge Problem

1.

2.

3.

(a)

(b)

Exercise 27-1A

GENERAL JOURNAL

PAGE

DATE		DESCRIPTION	POST. REF.	DEBIT	CREDIT

Exercise 27-2A

Name ________________________________

Exercise 27-3A

GENERAL JOURNAL

PAGE

DATE		DESCRIPTION	POST. REF.	DEBIT	CREDIT

Exercise 27-4A

GENERAL JOURNAL

PAGE

DATE		DESCRIPTION	POST. REF.	DEBIT	CREDIT

Exercise 27-5A

GENERAL JOURNAL

PAGE

	DATE		DESCRIPTION	POST. REF.	DEBIT	CREDIT	
1							1
2							2
3							3
4							4
5							5
6							6
7							7
8							8
9							9
10							10
11							11
12							12
13							13
14							14
15							15
16							16
17							17
18							18
19							19
20							20
21							21
22							22
23							23
24							24
25							25
26							26
27							27
28							28
29							29
30							30
31							31
32							32
33							33
34							34
35							35

Problem 27-6A

1.

	A	B	C	D	E	F	G	H	I
1	Lundberg Company								
2	End-of-Period Spreadsheet								
3	For Year Ended December 31, 20--								
4	ACCOUNT TITLE	TRIAL BALANCE		ADJUSTMENTS				ADJUSTED TRIAL BALANCE	
5		DEBIT	CREDIT		DEBIT		CREDIT	DEBIT	CREDIT
6	Cash	30,300.00							
7	Government Notes	5,000.00							
8	Interest Receivable								
9	Accounts Receivable	34,000.00							
10	Allow. for Doubtful Accounts		530.00						
11	Finished Goods Inventory	24,000.00							
12	Work in Process Inventory	9,000.00							
13	Materials Inventory	8,500.00							
14	Estimated Returns Inventory	60.00							
15	Office Supplies	3,100.00							
16	Factory Supplies	3,800.00							
17	Land	100,000.00							
18	Factory Building	120,000.00							
19	Accum. Depr.—Factory Build.		10,000.00						
20	Factory Equipment	40,000.00							
21	Accum. Depr.—Factory Equip.		5,000.00						
22	Accounts Payable		13,800.00						
23	Customer Refunds Payable		120.00						
24	Income Tax Payable								
25	Interest Payable								
26	Bonds Payable		80,000.00						
27	Capital Stock		50,000.00						
28	Paid-In Capital in Excess of Par		30,000.00						
29	Retained Earnings		92,820.00						
30	Cash Dividends	30,000.00							
31	Sales		410,720.00						
32	Sales Returns and Allowances	6,100.00							
33	Interest Revenue		300.00						
34	Factory Overhead	78,630.00	89,300.00						
35									
36									
37									
38	Cost of Goods Sold	190,700.00							
39									
40	Wages Expense	70,000.00							
41	Office Supplies Expense								
42	Bad Debt Expense								
43	Utilities Expense—Office	4,400.00							
44	Interest Expense	7,000.00							
45	Income Tax Expense	18,000.00							
46		782,590.00	782,590.00						
47									
48									

Problem 27-6A (Continued)

2. a.

Problem 27-6A (Continued)

b.

c.

Problem 27-6A (Continued)

d.

Problem 27-6A (Concluded)

Problem 27-7A

1.

Problem 27-7A (Continued)

2.

Problem 27-7A (Continued)

3.

Problem 27-7A (Concluded)

Problem 27-8A

1.

GENERAL JOURNAL

PAGE

	DATE	DESCRIPTION	POST. REF.	DEBIT	CREDIT	
1						1
2						2
3						3
4						4
5						5
6						6
7						7
8						8
9						9
10						10
11						11
12						12
13						13
14						14
15						15
16						16
17						17
18						18
19						19
20						20
21						21
22						22
23						23
24						24
25						25
26						26
27						27
28						28
29						29
30						30
31						31
32						32
33						33
34						34
35						35

Problem 27-8A (Continued)

2.

GENERAL JOURNAL

PAGE

	DATE		DESCRIPTION	POST. REF.	DEBIT	CREDIT	
1							1
2							2
3							3
4							4
5							5
6							6
7							7
8							8
9							9
10							10
11							11
12							12
13							13
14							14
15							15
16							16
17							17
18							18
19							19
20							20
21							21
22							22
23							23
24							24
25							25
26							26
27							27
28							28
29							29
30							30
31							31
32							32
33							33
34							34
35							35

Problem 27-8A (Concluded)

3.

GENERAL JOURNAL

PAGE

DATE		DESCRIPTION	POST. REF.	DEBIT	CREDIT

Exercise 27-1B

GENERAL JOURNAL

PAGE

DATE		DESCRIPTION	POST. REF.	DEBIT	CREDIT

Name ______________________________

Exercise 27-2B

Exercise 27-3B

GENERAL JOURNAL

PAGE

	DATE	DESCRIPTION	POST. REF.	DEBIT	CREDIT	
1						1
2						2
3						3
4						4
5						5
6						6
7						7
8						8
9						9
10						10
11						11
12						12
13						13
14						14
15						15
16						16
17						17
18						18
19						19
20						20
21						21
22						22
23						23
24						24
25						25
26						26
27						27
28						28
29						29
30						30
31						31
32						32
33						33
34						34
35						35

Exercise 27-4B

GENERAL JOURNAL

PAGE

	DATE		DESCRIPTION	POST. REF.	DEBIT	CREDIT	
1							1
2							2
3							3
4							4
5							5
6							6
7							7
8							8
9							9
10							10
11							11
12							12
13							13
14							14
15							15
16							16
17							17
18							18
19							19
20							20
21							21
22							22
23							23
24							24
25							25
26							26
27							27
28							28
29							29
30							30
31							31
32							32
33							33
34							34
35							35

Exercise 27-5B

GENERAL JOURNAL

PAGE

DATE		DESCRIPTION	POST. REF.	DEBIT	CREDIT

Problem 27-6B
1.

	A	B	C	D	E	F	G	H	I
1	Woods Company								
2	End-of-Period Spreadsheet								
3	For Year Ended December 31, 20--								
4	ACCOUNT TITLE	TRIAL BALANCE		ADJUSTMENTS				ADJUSTED TRIAL BALANCE	
5		DEBIT	CREDIT		DEBIT		CREDIT	DEBIT	CREDIT
6	Cash	28,400.00							
7	Government Notes	6,000.00							
8	Interest Receivable								
9	Accounts Receivable	32,800.00							
10	Allow. for Doubtful Accounts		610.00						
11	Finished Goods Inventory	26,100.00							
12	Work in Process Inventory	10,200.00							
13	Materials Inventory	9,300.00							
14	Estimated Returns Inventory	65.00							
15	Office Supplies	4,200.00							
16	Factory Supplies	8,600.00							
17	Land	80,000.00							
18	Factory Building	160,000.00							
19	Accum. Depr.—Factory Build.		30,000.00						
20	Factory Equipment	60,000.00							
21	Accum. Depr.—Factory Equip.		20,000.00						
22	Accounts Payable		16,000.00						
23	Customer Refunds Payable		125.00						
24	Income Tax Payable								
25	Interest Payable								
26	Bonds Payable		100,000.00						
27	Capital Stock		60,000.00						
28	Paid-In Capital in Excess of Par		20,000.00						
29	Retained Earnings		111,400.00						
30	Cash Dividends	40,000.00							
31	Sales		404,680.00						
32	Sales Returns and Allowances	5,040.00							
33	Interest Revenue		500.00						
34	Factory Overhead	81,590.00	92,300.00						
35									
36									
37	Cost of Goods Sold	198,300.00							
38	Wages Expense	78,700.00							
39	Office Supplies Expense								
40	Bad Debt Expense								
41	Utilities Expense—Office	4,900.00							
42	Interest Expense	9,000.00							
43	Income Tax Expense	12,420.00							
44		855,615.00	855,615.00						
45									
46									

Problem 27-6B (Continued)

2. a.

Problem 27-6B (Continued)

b.

c.

Problem 27-6B (Continued)

d.

Problem 27-6B (Concluded)

Problem 27-7B

1.

Problem 27-7B (Continued)

2.

Problem 27-7B (Continued)

3.

Name ______________________________

Problem 27-7B (Concluded)

Problem 27-8B

1.

GENERAL JOURNAL

PAGE

DATE		DESCRIPTION	POST. REF.	DEBIT	CREDIT

Problem 27-8B (Continued)

2.

GENERAL JOURNAL

PAGE

	DATE		DESCRIPTION	POST. REF.	DEBIT	CREDIT	
1							1
2							2
3							3
4							4
5							5
6							6
7							7
8							8
9							9
10							10
11							11
12							12
13							13
14							14
15							15
16							16
17							17
18							18
19							19
20							20
21							21
22							22
23							23
24							24
25							25
26							26
27							27
28							28
29							29
30							30
31							31
32							32
33							33
34							34
35							35

Problem 27-8B (Concluded)

3.

GENERAL JOURNAL

PAGE

	DATE		DESCRIPTION	POST. REF.	DEBIT	CREDIT	
1							1
2							2
3							3
4							4
5							5
6							6
7							7
8							8
9							9
10							10
11							11
12							12
13							13
14							14
15							15
16							16
17							17
18							18
19							19
20							20
21							21
22							22
23							23
24							24
25							25
26							26
27							27
28							28
29							29
30							30
31							31
32							32
33							33
34							34
35							35

Mastery Problem

1.

Mastery Problem (Continued)

2.

Mastery Problem (Continued)

3.

Mastery Problem (Continued)

4.

GENERAL JOURNAL

PAGE

DATE		DESCRIPTION	POST. REF.	DEBIT	CREDIT

Mastery Problem (Concluded)

GENERAL JOURNAL

PAGE

	DATE		DESCRIPTION	POST. REF.	DEBIT	CREDIT	
1							1
2							2
3							3
4							4
5							5
6							6
7							7
8							8
9							9
10							10
11							11
12							12
13							13
14							14
15							15
16							16
17							17
18							18
19							19
20							20
21							21
22							22
23							23
24							24
25							25
26							26
27							27
28							28
29							29
30							30
31							31
32							32
33							33
34							34
35							35

Challenge Problem

1.

GENERAL JOURNAL

PAGE

	DATE		DESCRIPTION	POST. REF.	DEBIT	CREDIT	
1							1
2							2
3							3
4							4
5							5
6							6
7							7
8							8
9							9
10							10
11							11
12							12
13							13
14							14
15							15
16							16
17							17
18							18
19							19
20							20

2.

Printed and bound by CPI Group (UK) Ltd, Croydon, CR0 4YY
14/09/2026
02216366-0001